My Garden's Choice

My Garden's Choice

OF ROCK PLANTS, TREES AND FLOWERING SHRUBS AND HERBACEOUS PLANTS

BY

THEO. A. STEPHENS *and* A. T. JOHNSON

*Containing 24 Colour Plates
and 144 Half-Tone Illustrations from
Photographs by A. T. Johnson*

LONDON

My Garden

34 SOUTHAMPTON STREET, STRAND
LONDON, W.C.2

FIRST IMPRESSION SEPTEMBER 1941

Printed in Great Britain by
Hazell, Watson & Viney, Ltd., London and Aylesbury

CONTENTS

Note.—In all cases where the name only appears under an illustration the detailed description, cultural notes, etc., will be found in the alphabetical list preceding the section.

FOREWORD

THE plan of this book has been in my mind for a long time, mainly because I have, so often in the past, found the need for such a work in my own gardening. More recently I began to think out the plan in detail and, finding I had a great deal of the material available, determined that I would proceed with the book if I could find a collaborator. I approached my friend, A. T. Johnson, with whom I have worked very closely for over ten years, and found he was equally enthusiastic as to the welcome such a book was likely to meet with, so together we proceeded to mature the plan and produce this present volume which we hope and believe will be of very real value to a wide circle of gardeners.

We had no intention at any time of attempting to make a complete catalogue of plants and trees in the three sections of the garden we cover. Our aim was to simplify the reader's problems by listing a comprehensive selection which we consider the best for general purposes : plants and trees which will not disappoint either because of mediocrity or undue " miffiness."

Our descriptions and cultural notes are brief, but we trust adequate for the purpose we have in mind.

The illustrations, which are the strong feature of this book, are all from photographs taken by A. T. Johnson.

THEO. A. STEPHENS.

ROCK GARDENS AND ROCK PLANTS

WE have always had rock gardens ever since ladies in hooped skirts and poke-bonnets, suitably beflowered, passed sunny afternoons with their exclusive quarter of the pleasance which they called their lapidium. But rock gardens, as we know them to-day, had not become a serious part of our horticultural round; they had not taken a grip of public imagination, nor induced every sort of garden owner to launch out into adventure with stones and alpines, until thirty or forty years ago. And so intensely did this new-found project come to stir the garden-minded that it very soon became an epidemic, leading, as one has learned, to all manner of grotesque extravagances in the handling of stones. These meaningless conglomerations we have not seen the last of yet, but there is, on the other hand, evidence in abundance to show that the object-lessons provided by Chelsea and other great shows have had a far-reaching influence among the general run of amateurs as to what a rock garden should be and look like. We have risen from the ridiculous to the sublime, and rock gardening, having found its feet, so to speak, pursues its way as a recognised feature of almost every garden, no longer floundering in a slough of amorphism but enjoying its rightful destiny as a very finished product with a definite purpose to fulfil.

And what is that purpose? Surely not an egregious massing together of rocks, as though mere rocks were the primary object in view. Nor yet an attempt to copy Nature's haphazard tumbling of her broken architecture. The purpose of a rock garden is to provide a congenial dwelling-place for appropriate plants, rocks being employed as a means of affording drainage, relieving too flat a contour with natural dignity and offering such association as is conducive to the welfare and setting of the plants used. An imitation of a stratified section of lime-stone, or a granite outcrop, in each case restrained so as to be within the scope of the environ-ment, may be delightful, but the piling-up of stones for stones' sake must be no less sternly suppressed than the erection of a miniature Matterhorn in a villa garden.

It has to be admitted that a rock garden is not the easiest thing to place in the average English garden, for it is so apt to create an incongruous effect. In small areas where there is little else this difficulty may not be so apparent, but in larger places one must have a care in the locating of it. As a rule, it is wisest to have the rock garden at some little distance from the house or close to it. What we must avoid is the sudden coming upon it from a walk among roses, or flowering shrubs and trees, and it belongs neither to the formal nor the informal lay-out. Needless to say, its position must be in the open, away from trees, and if it is, as suggested, some way from the house the track to it may well consist of such a planting that will lead one to it gradually instead of abruptly. Thus from a plantation of trees one may pass to shrubs, from shrubs to lesser shrubs in the way of heaths, double gorse, brooms, dwarf conifers and pernettyas, with here and there a bold and picturesque rock, or stone trough or two, placed in a prominent position along the walk. So one approaches the rock garden with a mind in a measure attuned for it, so that it will appear in the scene with a sympathetic fitness.

Building a rock garden is an expensive operation—unless of course it is thrown in by the contractor who built the house, which heaven forbid! But this obstacle need not prevent anyone from enjoying the company of rock plants, for it is quite possible to grow a vast number of varieties in beds without any rocks at all, or at most a very few sunken to two-thirds of their depth. Such beds, made of well-drained gravelly loam with some rubble worked in and a good dressing of ½-in. chips, will do for almost anything and, incidentally, prove extremely labour-saving. An open situation is essential, and rock beds of this description are so unlikely to disagree with the tone of their environment that they can be accommodated in formal gardens, on the lawn or the terrace. They should not be too mounded-up, just a moderate lift above the general level, and may be of any desired shape.

Rock beds, when in formal surroundings, including terraces, harmonise very amicably with that comparatively new departure, the stone trough. As a receptacle for alpines, the more difficult and smaller ones in particular, this has been extraordinarily successful, and if ancient hand-wrought stone pig-troughs, antique sinks, water cisterns and the like are carefully chosen for their artistic merit and old-world design they will take their place in any formal or semi-formal lay-out—or, as suggested, in the approach to the rock garden itself—with remarkable appropriateness. All that they require is a hole or two for drainage, a liberal " crocking " at the bottom and a filling with any good and gritty rock-garden compost, the whole being well firmed and topped with chips or coarse grit. A few stones of taking shape may be sunk in the compost with their noses protruding, this to relieve a too even surface ; but rather than build a giddy peak on the trough we would have no stones at all. Watering, which will be essential in dry summer weather, is greatly facilitated by a flat surface, and if the gravelled top of the compost does not rise quite to the rim of the trough so much the better. It is possible to grow a large number of carefully selected little plants in one or two of these receptacles and so derive a great deal of fun and interest with a minimum of anxiety. Indeed, we know of no home for alpines which can be maintained so successfully with such an absence of care as these trough gardens.

It is probably in these recommendations offered by the stone trough that we shall discover the secret fascination of the rock garden itself. To put the matter more clearly, is not the fact that the growing of alpines (we use the word in its broadest sense) enables us to possess and enjoy more plants to a given area than any other phase of horticulture one of the primary factors in securing the popularity of rock gardening? Then if the stone trough affords us that close-up intimacy with its inmates which is so intriguing—incidentally, since it will be raised, saving us a deal of backache—the rock garden exerts the same intimacy only to a less sensitive degree. In the matter of maintenance again, that troublesome problem which most of us have to face, the stone trough's immunity as a source of worry is no more than an epitome of what we find in the rock garden. There are grousers, we are aware, who contend that the latter is not labour-saving. But it is our experience that there are few garden features which need so little in the way of attention as a rock garden. You can promote trouble, of course, by planting unruly or unsuitable things, by having too much of those grassy sweeps which look so nice in some of the show pieces, by going in for too much bog or waterside planting and by attempting more in a general way than you can well manage. But, given a rock garden of dimensions to suit your resources, let it be stocked with well-tried, well-behaved plants and shrubs, not forgetting those that will naturalise by sowing themselves, and we contend that the demands it will make on your time will be negligible.

There is yet another phase of this extensive subject which is even more immune from care, that can, indeed, practically be left to its own devices, and that is the alpine lawn. On an easy, sunny slope of light, stony soil, preferably, but not necessarily, a part of the rock garden, this can be something more than a solace to the idle (or busy), for, enveloped by a close-fitting jacket of creeping thymes, prostrate brooms, raoulias, antennarias and mat-forming dianthus, it presents a beautiful array of charming colours which even in the off-season will be a tapestry of changeful greens and greys. In principle this sward of ground-hugging plants, relieved here and there by a few tufted ones of suitable character, so cover the soil that weeds are excluded and moisture retained. And in practice it works out exceedingly well and can be an object of perennial beauty in a quiet way and a blessed relief from all cultural aid.

Much of the success of rock gardening depends, as we have inferred, upon the choice of plants, and while it is not for us to deter the enthusiast from experimenting with the rare and temperamental, knowing something of the " kick " to be got out of such ventures—when they succeed—the everyday rock gardener will be wise who banks on plants of established reputation for his main furnishing. These are plants—we all know them—which have stood the test of time as good doers under average conditions, plants that winter well, that are reasonably permanent and, not least, possessed of real merit. We have in mind such trustworthy standbys as Campanula Portenschlagiana, Alyssum saxatile, Primula marginata and Dianthus arvernensis, plants that will enrich any rock garden with beauty and interest and never give one cause for a moment's concern as to their welfare.

However, there is, as we have hinted, another side to the matter, most of us sooner or later developing the urge to dandle with the difficult, to pit our patience and skill against problems which call forth the best that is in us if we are to overcome them. And we are ready to grant that the gamble has its rewards. Man cannot live by aubrietia alone. He must indulge his sporting instinct by engaging in combat with the dourness of Gentiana Farreri, with the nostalgia of Primula Allionii. And if he succeeds his triumph is warming to the soul. He has added another stone to our temple of knowledge, and the process, if bitter at times, has afforded him an engrossing interest which is as good for him as it is good for gardening. So it is with the new plant. The thrill of growing something that has never before opened its petals to an English sky is something to live for. The slow discovery of its likes and dislikes has the quality of a romantic story. Wherefore, while still adhering to the principle of making the recognised and generally reliable the main complement of the garden, there is a deal to be said on behalf of ventures in the more conflicting country of the wayward and rare.

There is, it seems, a prevalent belief that having the right soil is the master-key to success in rock gardening. But experience very quickly teaches us that there is no such thing as a right soil, even for a single plant. We do not know why one can grow and flower Gentiana acaulis to perfection and why another, under what appear to be exactly similar conditions, fails to do any good with it. We know a man who could not grow aubrietia with any success, and those of us who have been entirely defeated over Gentiana Farreri may be raised to pinnacles of envy by seeing drifts of its incomparable blue in somebody else's garden which, to all appearances, has a soil just like our own. Why, we have even heard of a well-known alpinist who grows to his entire satisfaction the whole range of rock plants, including many of the least tractable, in a stiff, clayey loam!

Is there, therefore, any excuse needed for our saying so little here about soils? The obvious conclusion is, we must all make our own discoveries as to what plants best suit our particular medium. We put it in that way knowing that it is infinitely wiser, on a broad view, to choose plants to suit the soil rather than to try to make the soil suit the plants. But there is, after all, this abiding comfort: most plants are extremely tolerant. They allow for considerable latitude, especially those standard kinds to which we have referred and which, for the most part, comprise the selection included in the following pages. Even over the question of lime there is a deal of unnecessary fussing. The ericaceæ (Erica carnea is the exception that proves the rule) cannot abide lime and the Chinese gentians do not like it. But the great bulk of rock plants, whether they come from calcareous regions or acid soils, can be expected to behave indifferently towards that much-discussed element or the absence of it.

Given a medium loam, inclined to the light side, with grittiness to promote friability, one may go ahead with confidence, applying humus in the way of leafmould for such as need it. But of greater importance than the composition of one's soil is the drainage. This must be sharp and efficient. It must not fail in the wettest of winter weather, and the freeness of the soil combined with plenty of depth which accelerates this seepage of water will, on the other hand, tend to promote the upward percolation of moisture from the deeps which makes for that uniformity in the supply of that necessity which most plants expect.

Now for a final word about rock-garden shrubs. These, of course, scarcely exist in the mind's eye of the alpine purist who visualises only those children of cloudland which must remain more or less cushioned and lowly and firm lest they be blown off their dizzy heights. But our rock gardens, being a happy blend of the higher plants and those of alpine meadow and sub-alpine regions of the tree-line, even of sea-level, include a number of the lesser shrubs which have a definite end to fulfil.

These rock shrubs may roughly be divided into two kinds, those which are merely evergreens and the flowering class. The latter, of course, contribute their share of colour, but they also, like the evergreens, play the equally important part of breaking up a level that might otherwise be too flat. The columnar and pyramidal ones are especially instrumental in "lifting" what may suffer from too much uniformity, but if carefully placed in commanding positions they also impart point and character to one's work, and in this the humpy ones will take a share in their own way. Yet another desirable feature in rock shrubs is that they are generally permanent. True, a good many of them eventually offend by outgrowing their quarters, dwarfing other things and disturbing the balance of the whole. But there are as many as any average garden needs which do not abuse the hospitality afforded them and which will remain indefinitely as key-features of interest and beauty. Then these shrubs, especially evergreens like the little conifers, dwarf rhododendrons and heaths, do more than anything else to endow a rock garden with a year-round interest and that atmosphere of maturity which is so desirable. They are, indeed, the most efficacious of all things in mellowing the raw. This they do quickly, and we are comforted during the long service they give by their hearty independence and freedom from care.

ROCK GARDEN PLANTS

A Selection for the Average Garden

AËTHIONEMA GRANDIFLORUM. A distinguished member of a popular family, a foot or more in height, with grey-green leaves and a sheaf of long flower heads in a rich and brilliant pink. Habit bushy and erect. A grand plant for a sunny cleft in light soil.

AË. WARLEY HYBRID. A garden hybrid, but one of the most beautiful. It forms a low, widespread bush of blue-grey leaves which is enveloped in the later spring with bright rose-pink flowers. Likes a light, stony soil and full sun. A close ally of the slightly rosier, W. Rose (see p. 49). Cuttings.

ALYSSUM SAXATILE CITRINUM (see p. 58). A variety of that grand old plant, A. saxatile, but more compact. It has the almost white leaves of golden alyssum but its billows of blossom are sulphur-yellow. A hot, dry crevice between boulders or in a sunny wall. Can be raised true from seed.

ANACYCLUS DEPRESSUS (see p. 65). A fairly recent introduction from the Atlas presenting a cartwheel of prostrate ferny growths terminating in pink and white daisies.   For gravel bed, scree or very gritty soil. Full sun.

ANDROSACE LANUGINOSA. Doubtless the most reliable of a short-lived race. In any light, gritty soil, with sun, it will weave wide mats of silvery, silky leafage and put up (summer and autumn) primula-like heads of lilac blossom.

A. SARMENTOSA. Close up to the foregoing in winning our confidence, this delightful plant adorns its silky rosettes with pink flowers, and it includes a pocket edition, Chumbyi, with more silvery leaves and blooms of a deeper pink. The variety, yunnanensis, is also a full-toned pink and it has a closer, less rambling habit. Any sunny slope of free soil will suit these pretty trailers. An occasional top-dressing with fine chips is helpful.

ANEMONE BLANDA. Preceding A. apennina (see p. 52) by at least two months, this adorable little 3-in. windflower greets the earliest spring with wide-rayed flowers ranging from a thin lavender to deepest violet, and there are pinks and a white. The white variety, scythinica, with a blue reverse, is very lovely. Any loam in full sun.

A. HEPATICA. See p. 41.

A. NEMOROSA ALLENII. Among the many wood anemones none is so distinguished as this. Taller than the rest, broader in leaf, larger in flower and without a peer in the luminous tone of its clarified lavender-blue, it is chieftain of the clan. Moreover, since it is the latest to flower, it prolongs the season of these delectable treasures and is easily grown in a medium loam, preferably with light shade.

A. N. ROBINSONIANA. Approaching Allenii in merit with a lovely lavender-blue around its wreath of gold. A trifle earlier than its rival and a first-rate all-round plant.

Among other desirable nemorosas are the Double White, Blue Bonnet, the pale blue Celestial and Royal Blue.

A. RANUNCULOIDES. A buttercup-yellow version of our native windflower, and equally agreeable as to site and soil. There is an especially good form, superba, and a pretty double.

A. SYLVESTRIS. The " Snowdrop Anemone " is like a miniature A. japonica with a running habit and gracious milk-white flowers nodding on 9-in. stems. The variety grandiflora (or Spring Beauty) is preferable to the type, and this is in bloom more or less all summer and autumn. A cool soil, away from treasures it is liable to overrun. Seed or division.

AQUILEGIA ARCTICA (FORMOSA). An elegant columbine of only 12 in. with dainty maidenhair leaves and gaily poised blossoms, nearly all summer, in scarlet and gold. Best left to occur from its own seed, which comes true. Any light soil.

A. CÆRULEA. A stately Rocky Mountain species bearing on erect 15-in. stems upturned, long-spurred blossoms, bright lavender-blue and creamy-white. One of the parents of our long-spurs. Any light, rich soil, full light. Seed.

A. LONGISSIMA. A very beautiful American of 2 ft. for associating with the larger occupants of any well-prepared rock-garden soil. Refined in foliage and eminently graceful, this newcomer carries throughout the later summer enormously long-spurred columbines in a brilliant yellow with amber shadings.

ARABIS AUBRIETIOIDES. Suggesting a frail and refined A. albida, but with rounder, more shapely blossoms, rosy lavender. A pleasant rock cress for trailing down a partly shaded slope and one that is perfectly easy anywhere.

A. BLEPHAROPHYLLA. A clumpy plant of some 6 in. with sprays of rose-purple blossoms in April. Needs winter care in most places. Seed, and selection for good colour forms is suggested.

ARENARIA BALEARICA. Familiar as a close moss-like film of green which in late spring becomes pricked with white stars on very short stems. A winning little mite for covering a boulder, or stone steps in shade, but not a plant to risk among one's more precious nuggets.

A. MONTANA. See p. 59.

ARMERIA CÆSPITOSA. A southern thrift, forming a spiny mound of a few inches which in spring is enveloped in almost stemless flowers in a silvery rose. A thin, hot soil, or a rock fissure, is what this little gem enjoys. There is a rather larger variant of this called superba, but mere size is a questionable virtue in such matters. Seed sown in a pan of gritty soil germinates freely.

A. MARITIMA. See p. 40.

ASPERULA SUBEROSA. A choice alpine for a sunny spot in sharply drained gravelly soil or scree. It forms a 4-in. hummock of fine leafage all swaddled in silky hairs, and this it covers in late spring with waxen trumpet flowers in a soft salmon-pink. It will be grateful for a pane of glass over it in winter where or when rain is excessive.

ASTER ALPINUS. See p. 48.

A. MARJORIE. This is one of the lowly, compact and prolific race of dwarf asters recently introduced. It does not exceed 9 in., and the flowers, over 1 in. and a clear silver-pink, are not at their best until October. A hardy, easy-going plant for any soil with full sun. It is readily increased by division (see p. 46).

A. THOMSONII NANA. A charming little aster of erect growth but only 9 in. or so. The leaves are a downy silver-green and the comparatively large blue-lilac flowers are borne throughout summer and autumn. A sunny site and a well-drained ordinary soil is all this choice plant asks.

ASTILBE CRISPA. A charming pigmy astilbe with a low bunch of crisp and curly leaves, deep metallic green, and over them 4–6-in. stocky, erect spires of white flowers about mid-summer. There are various colour forms—Daumlung, rose; Gnome, pink; Kobald, rose-pink; Lilliput, blush; Perkoë, pale pink. These fascinating little creatures are easily grown and long-lived in a bed of cool, humous soil; sun or light shade. Careful division, early spring.

A. SIMPLICIFOLIA. An exquisite dwarf of a stalwart race making a loose 4-in. tuft of undivided leaves and yielding in full summer fragile airy plumes of 6–8 in. scintillating with an iridescence of rose and white. A moist but well-drained bed of sandy loam and leafmould for this Japanese gem. Increase may be effected by division in spring or by seed.

AUBRIETIA. This excellent old rock plant may not thrill the alpine purist, but to the average rock gardener it makes a strong appeal on account of its unchanging good temper and the splendid masses of colour it produces with a minimum of care. A good selection should include Carnival, deepest purple; Church Knowle, soft lavender; Dr. Mules, bright violet-purple; Fire King Improved, vivid crimson; Gloriosa, very large-flowered clear rose; Lavender, delicate lavender-blue; Red Carnival, richest crimson, non-fading; Studland, lavender; Vindictive, large-flowered warm crimson.

AZALEA HINOMAYO. Among the many Japanese azaleas so admirable for rock gardens this variety can challenge any of them in the luxuriance of its flowering and the brightness and purity of its warm pink blossoms. It seldom exceeds 1 ft. with a spread of 2–3 ft., and is quite happy in any average lime-free soil (see p. 47).

Other dwarf azaleas, all first-rate shrubs of about the same height and needing the same treatment, include: Caldwellii, pale pink hose-in-hose; Fosteriana, semi-double warm crimson; Hinodegiri, bright red-crimson; H. O. Carre, semi-double pink; John Cairns, vivid tawny crimson; Kirin, deep rose; Illuminator, later, 3 ft., brilliant pink; Zampa, glowing terra-cotta red. (See also Shrub section.)

CALLUNA VULGARIS. Our native ling excels in varieties, many of which are most suitable for rock gardens. A choice of the medium to dwarf growers should include Camla, double pink; Carlton, a very fine "white heather"; J. H. Hamilton, double rose-pink, semi-prostrate, an excellent variety; Mullion, a stocky, freely branched rose-lilac. All these may be expected to thrive in a moderately moist free loam (without lime) with a little humus added at planting time. Full exposure. Such varieties as the above can be raised from short late summer cuttings.

CAMPANULA CARPATICA. An invaluable bellflower with 6–12-in. stems rising from a wide woody clump, and large bowl-shaped flowers nearly all summer. Many varieties.

white, purple, violet, lavender and lilac. Flourishes in any good loam. Increased easily by division (see p. 50).

C. HAYLODGENSIS. A neat 4-in. hybrid from the above (and perhaps pusilla) with pale green leaves and ample harebell-blue bells. Very useful as a late summer bloomer. Its double form (see p. 42) is distinctly attractive and lasts long in flower. Ordinary soil; sun or light shade.

C. ROTUNDIFOLIA JENKINSÆ. One of the best garden developments of our native harebell with fine fat bells on 8-in. stems in full summer. A deserving plant for a prominent sunny position (see p. 38).

C. ROT. OLYMPICA. Another of the harebell group and a first-rate plant with wide nodding bells of bright blue on 9-in. stems. All campanulas of this section are willing and permanent under the usual rock-garden conditions.

C. PORTENSCHLAGIANA (MURALIS). An old favourite and still perhaps the best of all rock-garden campanulas. A semi-trailing, bushy plant with glossy, evergreen leaves and sumptuous violet bells nearly all summer and autumn. Most adaptable as to soil and situation.

C. POSCHARSKYANA. A vigorous trailer for the bolder parts of the rock garden, rioting in a glorious tangle of long, slender branches, downy leaves and constellations of lavender stars. Any soil. Useful as a ground cover for dwarf shrubs.

C. PROFUSION. A 4-in. compact semi-trailer, this well-known hybrid, with its clear pale blue cup-shaped flowers, is one of the most precious of rock-garden bellflowers—and sweet-tempered under any conditions.

C. PULLOIDES. With larger flowers and a sounder constitution than C. pulla, this hybrid is an improved edition of the latter. Its big cup-shaped flowers on 3-in. stems are an intense violet, and culture is easy in a light loam, not too dry.

C. PUSILLA. All members of this group are lovely little bellflowers, easy to grow anywhere, always bright and happy and prodigal in their yield of fairy-bells. These latter, normally clear lavender-blue, with a charming white, touch their highest note in the beautiful Miss Willmott, a peculiarly luminous blue, and Miranda, whose tubby bells are an attractive blend of pale lavender and french-grey.

CARDAMINE PRATENSIS FL. PL. The best form of the double "Lady's Smock" is a beautiful rock plant for any coolish soil with sun. It puts up a bouquet of 9-in. stems bearing stock-like trusses of lilac blossoms in May.

CASSIOPE SELAGINOIDES. See p. 60.

CERATOSTIGMA PLUMBAGINOIDES. A creeping plumbago with erect 8-in. leafy growths crowned with flowers of purest blue in autumn followed by brilliant foliage tints. A good low shrub for a dry, poor soil; full sun. Division.

CHEIRANTHUS ALPINUS. A cheerful, contented little alpine wallflower, covering its mat of lively green in spring with golden-yellow flowers. Aurantiacum is the same thing in orange and a plant that deserves to be more widely grown; Moonlight is another variety with pale lemon flowers. These are happy enough in a sunny spot with some free gritty soil beneath them. The two colour forms mentioned should be raised from cuttings, the type from seed.

C. CHEIRI. The best double wallflower for rock gardens is the old Harper Crewe (Miss Hope), a compact, bushy plant of no more than 18 in. in a poor, dry soil—this being helpful in wintering and prolonging life. It bears in May and June long tapering spikes of very fragrant, rich golden-yellow " buttons " and may be propagated by cuttings.

C. MUTABILIS. Under this name we have a number of low-growing but widespread wallflowers in weird blends of buff, lilac, crimson, purple and bronzy maroon. These, which flower very freely, are singularly effective and most useful for introducing a contrasting note. E. K. Elmhurst is a somewhat newcomer of a foot in height with flowers in a taking shade of rose-lavender. All these wallflowers enjoy a taste of lime in the soil, but this is not essential.

CISTUS. Most of the true cistuses are too large for rock gardens and too tender for all but our milder localities. But for a back row in poor soil accommodation may be found for the rosy shrimp-pink C. Silver Pink, and the rich rose-red Sunset, a variety of C. crispus, is recommended. C. lusitanicus, with large white flowers blotched with crimson, is semi-procumbent, tolerably hardy and very beautiful, and the grey-leaved albidus with wide salvers of silvery mauve is another possible beauty. C. salvifolius, with sage-like leaves and pure white blossoms, is also good, but in this species we strongly advise for rock gardens the minia-ture, almost prostrate form lately introduced, an admirable shrub and uncommonly hardy. All need full sun, preferably a stony root-run, and they are increased by late summer cuttings.

CONVOLVULUS CNEORUM. A soft-wooded shrub of a foot or two, much taller and 3-4 ft. wide in seaside gardens. The narrow leaves glisten with a silver sheen, and the funnel-shaped flowers, over an inch across, are white flushed with pink. A beautiful shrub for a sunny nook, the soil being to the lean side. Cuttings.

C. MAURITANICUS. One of the best of all rock plants but not too hardy. It sends forth in the late summer yard-long trailing growths which produce wide bowl-shaped blossoms in a rich blue-violet. Good drainage, light soil and full sun. Being a late bloomer it may be used for cascading lightly over such plants as aubrietia which are closed down. Reserve cuttings should be wintered in a cold frame.

CORNUS CANADENSIS. See p. 44.

CORONILLA CAPPADOCICA. A pretty 4-in. plant with a semi-trailing glaucous foliage tipped with coronets of golden pea-flowers all summer. A warm but not too dry soil; sun or light shade.

CROCUS TOMASINIANUS. See p. 39.

CYCLAMEN COUM. This winter bloomer is a priceless gem for a thinly shaded spot and moist leafy soil. From December onwards it enlivens its sullen green leaves with puckish little blossoms in a brilliant carmine-rose and there is a delightful snow-white variety (see p. 46).

C. NEAPOLITANUM. See p. 45.

C. REPANDUM. A spring bloomer, with sprightly, long-petalled blossoms in a vivid ruby-crimson. An easy doer in most soils and sites, preferably part shade. May be grown in a cool fissure between rocks.

CYTISUS ARDOINII. Perhaps the most beautiful of the earlier rock brooms, making a loose downy carpet, a foot or so across and 4–6 in. high. This it adorns with a wealth of richly golden blossoms. Should have a poor gravelly soil with all possible sun.

C. DECUMBENS. A prostrate broom forming a dense mat of overlapping twigs which, in May or June, is ablaze with ½-in. yellow flowers. C. procumbens is in the same mode but taller and bushier. Both will cover a width of 3 ft. or so. Treatment as above.

C. LEUCANTHUS. This 8-in. mat-forming broom is useful inasmuch as it flowers towards the later summer when it covers its rich green with ivory-yellow clusters (see p. 56).

C. PURPUREUS. A low-growing, loose-habited shrub with purple pea-flowers. The best form is albo-carneus (incarnatus) in which the large blossoms are a bright rose. This and the last-mentioned appreciate a rather better soil than most brooms.

DABOËCIA CANTABRICA. See p. 61.

DAPHNE BLAGAYANA. A creeping, prostrate alpine yielding (February and March) posies of ivory-white, very fragrant flowers in a leafy rosette. Needs a flat, cool bed of sandy loam, leafmould and old peat in light shade, with a mulch of the same mixture in April.

DAPHNE CNEORUM. The loveliest of all rock shrubs, presenting a mound of olive-green, 1–3 ft. across, and in spring clusters of bright rose-pink blossoms, wonderfully fragrant. Capricious in its likes and dislikes but generally satisfied with a free loam containing a little humus. Full sun and an occasional mulch of sandy loam and leafmould. D. C. eximia is the finest variety, larger in all its parts and more richly coloured (see p. 47).

D. PETRÆA. A woody, close-set little shrub of a few inches with a crisp dark green foliage and large rose-pink flowers, waxen in texture and richly fragrant. An indispensable rock shrub and one to be tried with confidence in the above compost, preferably with the roots between two limestone blocks (see p. 67).

DIANTHUS BOYDII. A hybrid from D. alpinus but a much better garden plant. From a low pad of overlapping dark green leaves it puts up a crowd of large pink blossoms with a fringed margin and a central zone of crimson freckling. Starting in May it will seldom be without flower until autumn. It is content with any good light soil and makes an excellent stone trough plant (see p. 50).

D. CÆSIUS. With its cushions of blue-grey foliage and large flat flowers on 6-in. stems, deliciously scented, the Cheddar pink wins its way into every rock garden and readily proves its reliability in any light soil, preferably stony. There are several good garden variations, and closely akin are D. arvernensis and La Bourbrille (see p. 62). The former, making dense low silvery mats, is flushed with pink in spring and the latter follows with a galaxy of short-stemmed rosy-cerise blossoms.

D. DELTOIDES SUPERBUS. The familiar maiden pink is known in many varieties, one of the best being D. d. superbus, a prostrate grower with leaves of a deep bronzy red and flowers of the intensest ruby-crimson. Any good soil will please this friendly old pink.

D. NEGLECTUS. A true alpine and one of the elect, this beautiful species is variable but always good. Its close pads of grassy leaves give rise in spring to large round and flat blooms in a brilliant rose-pink with a buff reverse and a dusky eye. A well-drained gritty soil, or scree, in full sun. This is an ideal inmate for a stone trough garden. Seed; special forms from cuttings.

D. SUPERBUS. This delightful sub-alpine makes about 9 in. and bears deeply fringed, very fragrant flowers in rose-lilac, pink or white. Not one of the choicest but worth a place for its scent alone. It likes a cooler place than most pinks, i.e. a decent loam. Seed.

D. SYLVESTRIS. Though wanting in scent this is a charming pink for a light soil in sun. A tall grower with fine big rose-pink blossoms, soft and pure in tone. Cuttings.

There is an endless number of excellent rock-garden hybrid pinks, many of the utmost value, many too much alike. Several well-known specialists have their own strains. A selection should include Ariel, deepest rose-carmine; Enid, carmine; F. W. Millard, large double crimson, fringed; Gloria, intense velvety crimson-scarlet; Highland Fraser, pale lilac-pink, ruby zone; Little Jock, lilac-rose; Mars, an all-season blood-red double; Spark, crimson-scarlet. All these will prosper in any gravelly soil with full exposure and they are easily raised from late summer cuttings.

DRYAS OCTOPETALA. See p. 43.

D. SUNDERMANNII. A hybrid between the above and D. Drummondii and a plant that will sometimes prove easy where the other is shy. It has the same creeping habit and evergreen leaves, but the flowers, yellow in the bud, are cream and inclined to bend over. Any cool soil in sun with low rocks for it to mound over.

ERICA CARNEA. Although this splendid semi-prostrate winter bloomer is normally too large for the average rock garden it has some dwarfer varieties which are admirable plants. These include Ruby Glow, bright ruby-red; Vivellii, crimson-purple, bronzy foliage; Atro-rubra, late-flowering, deep pink; and the white Cecilia M. Beale. Should space allow for varieties with a spread of 3–5 ft., Springwood, the finest white; Springwood Pink, bright rose; King George, dark rose-lilac; and the pink Queen Mary will give a handsome return in winter-spring colour. A light sandy loam will suit this superb and very hardy heath, and it is one of the few ericas that will do in a limy soil.

E. CILIARIS. An outstanding form of the Dorset heath is Mrs. C. H. Gill, a shapely bushling of 8 in. carrying a luxuriant head of brilliant rose-red bells in late summer and autumn. Another excellent variety of this species is E. c. globosa with a greyish foliage and erect spikes of deep pink bells. The finest white is E. c. Stoborough.

E. CINEREA. The familiar bell-heather offers several good rock-garden sorts, one of the best being E. c. coccinea, an early bloomer of flattish growth with glowing red-crimson spikes. E. c. atrorubens, a trifle later and larger, has the same warm colouring, and E. c. carnea is a first-rate pink. The compact, low-growing E. c. Mrs. Dill with deep green foliage and rosy-carmine bells is also a most desirable rock heath.

E. HYBRIDA. This section includes the variety Dawn, 9 in., rich rose-red; H. Maxwell, 1 ft., bright pink; and the rather smaller Watsonii, all such prolific bloomers that they will not be out of colour from June to October. E. h. Darleyensis must also be included here. A bosky, 2-ft. shrub (carnea+mediterranea) it will not be without its shell-pink flowers from December to May.

E. MEDITERRANEA. One of the tree-heaths, but it gives us in dwarfs the excellent Brightness, 18 in., with rich rose-red bells, and the new W. T. Rackliff. The finest white of this section, the latter is not more than about 2 ft. and begins flowering in early March to carry on to May.

E. TETRALIX. Rather earlier in flowering than the common bell-heather, this closely allied heath makes compact little bushes of about a foot and in most varieties the foliage is a frosty grey-green. E. T. Lawsoniana is one of the most silvery, a mat-former with flesh-pink flowers. E. T. mollis, also powdery white, has round white bells, and Pink Glow, a charming variety, is the same thing with spikes of shell-pink. Then, for later flowering, there is the red-belled rubra.

All these heaths, with the exception of E. carnea, require a lime-free soil. A light but moderately moist medium suits them best, with full sun. Peat is not necessary, but they may be given a dash of moss peat, vegetable compost or leafmould at planting time. Increase of special varieties is carried out by short summer cuttings.

ERINUS ALPINUS. The ideal rock plant, content with no more than a rock fissure or wall crevice, whence it may seed where it will. The little cluster of green rosettes bristles with 3-in. sprays of rose-lilac blossoms in spring and at intervals through summer. There is a good white variety, a ruby-red (Dr. Haenaele) and the large-flowered Abbottswood Pink, a recent arrival of great merit.

ERODIUM. These cousins of the geraniums are beautiful plants for a well-drained gritty loam, with sun. One of the loveliest is E. chrysanthum with short flights of yellow over its silvery, fern-like foliage. E. macradenum is slightly larger, 6 in. or so, with greener leaves of the same fine cut and rose-lilac flowers with maroon blotches. E. trichomanifolium, about the same size, also ferny-leaved, has pale lilac blooms lined with purple. Then in a class by itself is the very lowly, broad-leaved, carpeting E. chamædryoides with white flowers, and a hybrid from it called E. hybridum roseum. This is in the same low and leafy style, but its flowers are rose, and of these it keeps up a supply all summer.

ERYSIMUM LINIFOLIUM. A rock wallflower of unusual quality with narrow, wavy leaves and blue-purple flowers. An excellent plant for dry, hot places and crevices into which it may be introduced by seed. Seldom exceeds 8 in. and is often semi-prostrate.

GENISTA DALMATICA. Like a miniature gorse of a few inches, but widespread, this charming broom gains our favour by holding off its golden yellow flowers until the later summer, when most of its kind are over.

G. HISPANICA. Rather large for all but extensive rock gardens, but its dense prickly mounds are extremely handsome when gilded with bright yellow flowers in spring. There is, for limited areas, a dwarfer variety, compacta, seldom exceeding 12–18 in., which can be unreservedly recommended. G. hispanica is a better garden shrub than its ally G. germanica.

G. JANUENSIS. An almost prostrate, dark-leaved broom bearing masses of rich yellow blossoms on its long straight branchlets in the later spring. Perhaps the most brilliant of its season.

G. PILOSA. Another still more prostrate broom of striking quality. It will creep over 2–3 ft. with its full-toned green, and this is lit in April with countless little golden blossoms. All these brooms are shrubs for a poor, dry soil and a sunny aspect.

G. SAGGITALIS. A trailer of only some 8 in. but eventually covering 2–3 sq. ft. with its dark metallic green, curiously winged branches. It puts up heads of downy yellow flowers on stalks of 4 in. and will thrive in any ordinary soil, with sun.

G. TINCTORIA PLENA. This is the best of the G. tinctoria group. A prostrate, dark green, neatly rounded mat, covered in summer with fully double blossoms which last longer than the singles. A sunny ledge of sandy loam serves for this bonny broom.

GENTIANA ACAULIS. A magnificent gentian with glorious trumpets, velvety in texture and of the deepest, purest blue. Not always a free bloomer in all soils, but will generally respond to a firm bed of tolerably stiff loam, rendered free by the use of grit and humus. Usually needs lifting, dividing and replanting, two or three crowns in a bunch, every third year. A top-dressing of leaf soil and grit brushed in with the hand in early spring is helpful. There is a white form and several affinities.

G. FARRERI. One of the loveliest of all gentians with a grassy foliage and big trumpets in a pure and vivid sky-blue. A temperamental plant in most gardens, but may be tried in a bed of sandy loam generously enriched with old leafmould. Summer moisture is essential, and it is said to appreciate lime, but on this point experiences do not agree.

G. SEPTEMFIDA. See p. 57.

G. SINO-ORNATA (see p. 51). One of the finest rock plants ever introduced. An autumn bloomer with large upstanding trumpets of brilliant sapphire, and willing to prosper in an average, non-limy, well-drained loam. Should be lifted and divided about every third year in spring. G. s. præcox is an early form commencing in July, and G. Macaulayi, a magnificent hybrid with all the virtues of sino-ornata, but larger flowers in a purer, more vivid blue.

G. VERNA. The despair of most of us, but too lovable a little plant to forgo. The variety angulosa, with equally brilliant and larger blue stars, is easier and can be tried with confidence in a deep bed of old leaf soil, grit, chunks of sandstone, sandy loam and old broken mortar, all made firm. Start with seedlings, not divided plants; keep moist in summer.

GERANIUM ARGENTEUM. A limestone cranesbill of the Eastern Alps, presenting a neat 4–6-in. tuft of gleaming silver foliage, and just above this comparatively large flowers in a clean pink, darkly veined. Gravelly soil, thorough drainage and sun. Perhaps safer in scree or a stone trough.

G. CINEREUM. Allied to the above but greener in leaf, and the pink flowers are not veined. There is an exquisite white variety. Same treatment as argenteum, and both may be increased by detaching short crowns and rooting them in pots of sandy soil.

G. ENDRESSII. A raspberry-pink Pyrenean of about 9 in. with a rhizomatous spread for the rougher parts of the rock garden. Flowers over a long period in summer and has yielded some pretty hybrids, silver- and flesh-pink, which are seldom out of bloom. Seed or division. Any soil or situation.

G. GRANDIFLORUM ALPINUM. This variety is a handsome plant for a partly shaded corner out of harm's way, for it creeps, but not rapidly. The nodding blossoms are bowl-shaped, 2 in. across, and a striking prussian-blue. Dwarfer and less invasive than the type. Light soil, preferably cool.

G. NAPULIGERUM. We refer here to the little cranesbill usually called G. Farreri. A choice alpine with the build and habit of argenteum, but larger flowers in a delicate rose-pink set off with black anthers. Not difficult in scree, or a free gritty loam in full sun. Seed is set and provides a ready means of increase.

G. NEPALENSE. Apparently an Asiatic kinsman of our sanguineum and a magnificent plant of about 1 ft. with deeply cut, broad downy leaves and rose-carmine flowers as big as half a crown. It is hardy and content with a free dryish loam in sun and easily increased by division of the rhizomes (p. 174).

G. PYLZOWIANUM. Much like Farrer's geranium, but it creeps by underground runners and bulbils. The flowers are large and a clear pink. Any light soil will satisfy it, but it should be put in a safe place, for in some gardens it is apt to become a nuisance. Division.

G. SANGUINEUM LANCASTRIENSE. This little native cranesbill is a first-rate rock plant, small, neat and easy to grow in any light soil with full sun. It covers its deeply cut leaves with 1-in. flowers in a thin blush-white with pink lines and will live for ever, asking no attention (see p. 68).

G. SUBCAULESCENS. A remarkable alpine cranesbill with leaves suggesting G. argenteum, but with lax stems of 9 in. or so bearing well-rounded blossoms the size of a shilling, dazzling carmine with a black eye. An easy doer in a free sandy soil.

G. RUSSELL PRICHARD. This cross between G. Traversii and G. sanguineum grows to about 6 in. with a spread of a foot or more. Its rather garish carmine-magenta flowers have a mollifying background in the silvery foliage and are yielded luxuriantly the season through. Ordinary light soil, with sun. Division.

GEUM. G. Borisii is another non-stop performer, and the blooms it lifts above its lowly bunch of leaves on 9-in. stems are a vehement scarlet. The golden-flowered G. montanum Ljuboten is another fine member of this family. G. reptans is also outstanding, with its prettily feathered foliage and big golden goblets, and for a cool soil G. rivale Leonard's Variety, or Jeannie Ross, with petals of old rose, are hard to resist. Most of the geums only ask the usual everyday soil and are generally amenable to increase by division.

GLOBULARIA. An interesting family of lowly alpines characterised by an evergreen foliage and fluffy heads of blossom in some shade of blue. Among the best and most reliable are G. bellidifolia; G. cordifolia, of which a pink and white form occur; G. nudicaulis, rather taller than the rest when in flower. Nice little plants for a sunny gravel bed or stone trough and generally quite reliable.

GYPSOPHILA CERASTIOIDES. One of the prettiest of alpines for a close-up position or trough. Its tuffet of downy leaves is only 2–3 in. high and bears in summer a galaxy of white flowers lined with pink. Quite permanent and responsive under average conditions. Careful division in spring.

G. FRATENSIS. A perfectly flat trailer spangled with pink flowers in early summer. Should be provided with a level bed, preferably gravelly, with a covering of chips to prevent soil splash. It enjoys sun but dislikes too dry a place.

G. REPENS. Another trailer that may be used for draping a sloping rock. Its prostrate growths are grey-leaved and in late spring are starred with white flowers, but there is a variety, rosea, with rather larger pink blossoms. A hearty plant under any reasonable treatment.

HABERLEA RHODOPENSIS. A cousin of ramondia and also a plant for a cool rock crevice which it will fill with its narrow, toothed leaves, and issue in April sprays of lavender-blue gloxinias. There is an exquisite white variety, Virginalis.

HALIMIOCISTUS SAHUCCII. Perhaps the best of all the lesser cistuses, this hybrid is a 1-ft. bush of ruddy, interlaced twigs 2 ft. across, with narrow deep green leaves, and this is sheeted in early summer with multitudes of 1-in. bowl-shaped white flowers. Light soil; full sun. Cuttings.

HALIMIUM LASIANTHUM. A grey-leaved rock rose with elegant trailing branches 2–3 ft. in length. The flowers which wreath these graceful branches in spring are the size of half a crown, bright yellow with an almost black zone round the central eye. A most beautiful shrub for leaning over a bold rock, and it has a self-coloured variety, concolor, which is worthy of it. Not the hardiest of plants, but generally safe in a really dry, meagre soil.

H. LIBANOTIS. Another of the yellow-flowered rock roses with almost linear leaves and spikes of rich yellow bowl-shaped blossoms. Height about 1–2 ft., inclined to trail. Poor soil; sun. Seed or cuttings.

H. UMBELLATUM. A semi-procumbent evergreen shrub with rosemary-like leaves and racemes of shapely little pure white flowers from spring onwards. Blooming nearly all the season through, hardier than most of its kindred and asking nothing more than the leanest of soils, this is a shrub to be welcomed to any rock garden.

HELIANTHEMUM. Confronted with the gay legions of the sun-roses we must unwillingly confine this brief notice to a mere mention of the dwarf perpetuals of the Ben group, and to a couple of others—H. croceum and H. rhodanthe carneum. The former bears large salver-shaped blossoms in a rich orange-yellow; the latter, broad of leaf and very silvery, has perhaps the biggest flowers of all, and they are a lovely rose, soft yet vivid. All things considered, this might claim to be the best of these sun-roses.

HUTCHINSIA ALPINA. A crucifer but a good one, raising a 4-in. mound of finely cut foliage, dark glossy green, which is smothered in spring with the whitest of little white flowers. Likes a cool side and does well in a rock cleft. Seed or division.

HYPERICUM CORIS. One of the brightest and most steadfast of its numerous family, this is a bristly heath-like bush of some 6 in., the very small leaves being glaucous, and it is crested during the later summer with 1-in. golden blossoms. Easily raised from seed and appreciates a thin soil and all possible sun.

H. GRANDIFLORUM. There being many " grandiflorums," this refers to that prostrate garden variety which suggests kinship with H. polyphyllum. The comparatively broad leaves are silver-grey, and the golden flowers, borne in profusion in late summer, are the largest of any rock-garden hypericum, being over 3 in. across. Can be increased by cuttings. Warm, light soil; full sun. Other first-rate hypericums in this class are repens and olympicum, with its pale lemon variety, citrinum.

H. REPTANS. A perfectly prostrate species, weaving an olive-green carpet, perhaps a yard wide, upon which appear in summer saucers of rich old gold which break from carmine-tinted buds. Enjoys rather cooler conditions than most, but a slope is preferable to the flat. Ordinary light, gritty soil. Soft cuttings taken in spring may be rooted.

IBERIS JORDANI. For places not spacious enough for the large white iberids this is a pleasing substitute. Its prostrate 4–6-in. purple growths, with dark green leaves, radiate cart-wheel fashion and bear at their upturned tips comparatively large milk-white flowers. An iberis of quality and one that does not find any light soil amiss.

I. SAXATILIS. Often called I. petræa, this is another of the minor rock candytufts suitable for a small garden or small spaces in big ones. A trim little plant with down-pressed woody branches, a yew-like foliage and heads of purest white in spring. Well-drained, gritty soil, or scree, with full exposure.

IRIS CRISTATA. A tiny flag iris with pale green leaves, only 3 in., and relatively large flowers in a clear blue-lavender and a golden crest. This most engaging mite enjoys a good loam, with lime and leafmould and shade from the hottest sun. Increased by detaching rooted rhizomes in spring.

I. GRACILIPES. Another fairy iris of exquisite grace, putting forth grassy fan-shaped leaf-sprays and 5-in. flights of flat blossoms about 1 in. across, lightly fringed, silken and the palest of lavender-blues with dainty elaborations of gold. A coolish bed of old peat, leafmould and sandy loam with protection from midday sun.

I. LACUSTRIS. A replica in miniature of the wee cristata and perhaps more free with its flowers. These doll's-house " flags " are only about 2 in. in height and a lively shade of blue-purple set off with a dash of gold. The same treatment as cristata, but can do with more sun.

I. RUTHENICA. Yet another of these baby irises, this one having grassy leaves of 6–8 in. in which nestle the dainty blue and white blossoms. I. ruthenica has a reputation for shy blooming, but the Transylvania form offered by some alpine specialists does not offend in this way. A gravelly bed with a little leafmould in not too hot a place.

JUNIPERUS COMMUNIS COMPRESSA. See p. 53.

LEUCOJUM VERNUM CARPATICUM. An advance on the familiar spring snowflake, with broader, glossier leaves and fuller bells of a good warm whiteness with an orange spot on each segment. These are spicily fragrant and the plant will naturalise in any average soil. A little later than the snowdrops. Height about 8 in. See p. 54.

LEWISIA HOWELLII. We find this one of the easiest of a pernickety race. From its flat and leathery rosette it raises tall, wide umbels of 1-in. starry blossoms in a charming blend of apricot and pink. A well-drained niche on a westerly slope, with sandy loam and old leaf soil, should suit this beauty, but it will thank you for a sheltering pane of glass in winter.

L. TWEEDYI. See p. 37.

LINARIA ALPINA. Possibly the most desirable of the family for the select rock garden, this more or less prostrate, glaucous-leaved plant of 3–4 in. will yield nearly all summer dainty snapdragons, violet with an orange lip. There are purple, rose and white varieties. Light soil, sun. A short-lived alpine, but it usually gives us self-sown seedlings.

LINNÆA BOREALIS. A lovely rambler for a shady side where it may thread its runners through dwarf ferns and the like. In summer these creeping branches emit pairs of nodding pink bells, almond-scented. The larger American form (canadensis) is more robust than our native. May be started in a pocket of lime-free sandy loam generously laced with leafmould.

LINUM ARBOREUM. A shrub of 1–2 ft. with grey-green leaves and a blaze of golden blossoms from May onwards. The hottest, driest and sunniest place, with a lean soil, for this cliff dweller of the south. L. flavum is a smaller edition in much the same format, but almost herbaceous.

L. MONOGYNUM. This hardy New Zealander raises an armful of graceful 2-ft. glaucous-leaved stems which are topped in summer with heads of wide white flowers. Makes a good background for the following variety. Not always hardy, even in the light warm soil it loves, but sets seed freely.

L. NARBONNENSE SIX HILLS. A magnificent development of the Narbonne flax presenting a tall sheaf of slender leaning stems with a long succession of large deep blue flowers with a satiny gloss. Hardy in most soils. Cuttings or rooted off-sets.

L. PERENNE. Another lovely flax of English soil, lighter in build than the foregoing and exceedingly gracious in its airy flights of sky-blue blossoms which prevail throughout the greater part of summer. Its height is about 20 in. Often seeds itself in a light, dryish soil. There are diversions in pale rose and white.

L. SALSOLOIDES NANUM. Here we have a semi-prostrate flax displaying a furry mat of needle-like foliage tipped with pearl-white dusky-eyed blossoms delicately pencilled with purple veins. A delightful thing for a free gritty soil, scree or stone trough; full sun.

LITHOSPERMUM GRAMINIFOLIUM. A sub-shrubby gromwell, tufty and grassy in foliage and raising in summer 8-in. stems, their tops leaning over in a cluster of brilliant blue bugles. Likes a stony cleft in moderately light soil; sun or part shade.

L. INTERMEDIUM. Probably a cross between the last-mentioned and L. petræum. A stronger grower than the former, with wider, glossier " grass " and bolder tassels of the same nodding bugles. Is at its best in cool, almost vertical crevices facing west. Both these gromwells can be increased by summer cuttings.

L. PROSTRATUM. Essential to every rock garden, this delightful trailer with its sombre verdure and flowers of " midnight blue " will be in bloom more or less from spring to autumn. The brighter and larger-flowered Heavenly Blue is the most favoured variety, and still bigger in blossom is the new Grace Ward. There is also the attractive and more bushy erectum, and a good white that runs well alongside the type. A broad, sunny, sloping ledge of gritty soil should satisfy this invaluable plant in all its forms.

LYCHNIS ALPINA. A pretty little closely tufted alpine and a rare native. It produces 3–4-in. stems with heads of pale magenta-rose in spring, and there are diversions in pink and white.

L. LAGASCÆ. A modest little catchfly with a recommendation for enduring a sun-baked arid soil, or rock fissure. It makes a 6-in. bush of grey-blue leaves and yields in summer a crowd of rosy stars. Both these catchflys may be raised from seed.

MACROTOMIA ECHIOIDES. The Prophet Flower always furnishes the rock garden with a note of interest, for it is generally uncommon, unlike anything else, and introduces yellow into a family (Borage) so often blue. From a tuft of hairy leaves the size of a prosperous primrose emerge 6-in. stems bearing ½-in. flowers in a rich yellow, each ornamented with five black-purple spots which gradually melt away as the blossom matures. A sound perennial, permanent in any average loam, not too heavy. Can be raised from seed.

MIMULUS LANGSDORFFII. Most of the mimulus are only suited to a rock garden that has a moist soil or waterside to offer them. For such a spot M. Langsdorffii is a useful carpeter, very generous with its blotched yellow flowers on 8–18 in. stems. An easy, showy plant, provided it has moisture enough. For drier spots, Whitcroft Scarlet.

M. LEWISII ALBA. The white variety of M. Lewisii is very charming and quite unique. It grows erect to about 6 in. and adorns its downy foliage with milk-white flowers, an unusual diversion in this family. A rather drier place in sandy loam with some humus should please this monkey-flower. It comes true from seed and often raises its own seedlings.

M. RADICANS. A creeping species with metallic bronzy-green overlapping leaves as compressed as a liverwort. This vegetable carpet becomes dappled with almost stemless pure white flowers with an orange centre and violet blotch. Any cool but well-drained moist soil in sun or light shade. Increases easily by division.

MOLKIA PETRÆA. Another of the Borage family and a near relation of lithospermum. A neat little bush of a foot or so with a greyish foliage and scrolls of tubular blue blossoms breaking from purple buds in summer. A plant for a warm, dry place with all available sun.

MORISIA HYPOGÆA. A lime-loving cress from Corsica which forms a humpy rosette of its glossy green, toothed leaves amid which nestle the brilliant yellow, almost stemless, blossoms. We find it permanent and happy in a sunny gravel bed over sandy loam, and it adorns a stone trough with success. Increased by root cuttings struck in sand.

MUSCARI BOTRYOIDES. Perhaps the most generally useful of the grape hyacinths, and best known in its variety Heavenly Blue. The crowded heads of richly scented globular bells vary from white (see p. 42) to the medium blue of the more typical. An early bloomer and ready naturaliser under most conditions.

M. ARMENIACUM. A grape hyacinth of superlative merit bearing, later than the above, bold 2–3-in. cones of blossom in a most brilliant blue on stems of 8 in. A plant for a place among the elect. Good deep soil; light shade.

M. LATIFOLIUM. An uncommon Grecian species well worth acquaintance, for it hoists above its broad twin leaves 9-in. stems, each knobbed with a cluster of bloom the size of a walnut, those at the lower part being black-purple, the upper ones a bright Cambridge blue.

M. PARADOXUM. An oddity among this fraternity, for it carries on each 10-in. stem a head of flowers in a blue so dark and dusky as to appear black. It sounds unattractive, but can be very striking against Aubrietia Dr. Mules or the whiteness of iberis. This and the above are quite content and permanent under the usual conditions.

MYOSOTIS ALPESTRIS. A true alpine forget-me-not and one of the most beautiful. The parent of many garden-raised forms which the exclusive alpinist would not admit. A variable plant, and the rock gardener who can secure the wild type of about 4 in. and make it happy in a gravel bed or scree should be well content, for it is a most delectable gem.

M. RUPICOLA. Another alpine, a rare native, and allied to alpestris, but lowlier and closer, with its squat huddle of little leaves which it crowns with blossoms on 2-in. stems in a brilliantly clear blue, a shade darker than that of its rival. Not an easy plant to keep but permanent enough in scree to earn one's confidence and loyalty.

MYRTUS NUMMULARIA. A delightful creeping myrtle weaving an evergreen mat with slender, red-barked, fishbone branches clothed with small, round, glossy leaves. White powder-puff flowers (summer) are followed by white, often pink-flushed, berries the size of marrowfat peas. This engaging shrub likes a cool root-hold and some low boulders to creep over. Cuttings or rooted branches.

NIEREMBERGIA RIVULARIS. Probably the best of the cup-flowers for rock-garden life. A creeping plant with a mat of leaves 1 in. high inset in late summer with pearl-white chalices. A sandy loam, moderately moist and sharply drained, should be provided for this striking curiosity.

ŒNOTHERA LINEARIS. Commonly known as Œ. riparia, this evening primrose is a brilliant little plant of 9–12 in., producing from a central crown a sheaf of slender stems, which throughout the summer is ablaze with golden-yellow blooms. Impatient of dryness, a coolish soil is desirable, with full sun.

Œ. TRILOBA. A tufted evening primrose with a long succession in summer of big vase-shaped, lemon-yellow blossoms. A non-trailer, it can be used where missouriensis and its allies may be troublesome. A sunny site and a light soil. Not long-lived but easily raised from seed.

OMPHALODES CAPPADOCICA. A 6-in. tufted member of the Borage tribe, having tongue-shaped glaucous leaves, and over these in spring it raises airy flights bearing $\frac{1}{2}$-in. forget-me-not flowers of an exquisite blue. A light, cool soil with part shade will make this charming plant comfortable and induce it slowly to colonise by seed and offset.

O. NITIDA. Another of the forget-me-not persuasion making a compact upright mass of long and narrow green leaves about 8 in. high, above which are borne nearly all summer delicately beautiful sprays of sky-blue blossoms. May be accorded the same treatment as the above. Self-sown seedlings may be picked up for increase.

OROBUS ALBO-ROSEA and O. TAURICA. A brace of the best and very striking plants for a warm, sunny spot or wall fissure. Both have silvery, downy leaves and top their 9-in. stems with tassels of drooping pear-shaped blossoms in summer, those of the former being white tipped with rose, of the other rich yellow. They need a free soil and dislike excessive winter wet.

OXALIS ADENOPHYLLA. One of the choicest of wood-sorrels with a swarm of crinkled glaucous leaves, and just above them the funnel-shaped blossoms, palest lilac-rose with a crimson eye, spread their wide petals. Any moderately moist, freely drained soil, with humus, will suit this beauty. Full sun is essential. Increased easily by division of the bulbs in the off-season (see p. 64).

O. ENNEAPHYLLA. With much the same leafage, rather bluer, the same funnel-shaped flowers, slightly smaller, and the same willingness to prosper indefinitely under similar conditions—with perhaps a trifle of shade—this lovely oxalis runs its rival close, if it does not eclipse it, and in addition to the pure glistening white of the type there are other colours running to pinks and, it is said, lilacs and mauves. Lift and divide when dormant every three or four years.

O. LOBATA. A most winsome bantling which puts forth in summer a handful of light green trefoils which soon die away. But in September they reappear accompanied by ½-in. flowers, shining like satin and a deep-toned gold. A sunny spot and gritty soil, or scree.

O. RUBRA. This is our old friend, O. floribunda, correctly named. A glorious plant when its scores of 9-in. stalks are bearing heads of gleaming carmine blossoms. It is quite easy under normal conditions, and its white variety is as valuable in its own way, for it is in flower the season through. Both are easily propagated by division of the tubers.

O. ROSEA. Though an annual, this will grace any rock garden with its 9-in. branching growths, bright green leaves and clusters of rose-pink. It seems to like a cool soil and some shade and commonly sows itself, but not excessively.

PAPAVER ALPINUM. This dainty elfin poppy is delightful for a warm, gritty soil in sun, or scree. Its pretty little crinkly bowls swing only 3–4 in. above the lowly pad of silvery leaves, and in colour they range from white to yellow, golden-orange, rosy-buff, salmon and fiery red. In a poor soil this imposing atom may live two or three seasons, but it is wisest to maintain one's stock annually by sprinkling a pinch of seed where the plants are to grow, that is, when there is not already plenty of self-sown seedlings.

PENTSTEMON NEWBERRYI RUPICOLA. See p. 55.

P. ROEZLII. The plant generally grown under this name is a semi-trailing, dwarf shrubby species with small leathery leaves, often bronzed, and short spikes of tubular flowers in a most daring ruby-red. A meagre soil and sunny aspect; does well in a rock cleft.

P. SCOULERI. A shrubby species and one which we find reliable among a host of mimps. It grows to about 15 in. with the best of manners, its leaves are glaucous and the large trumpet-flowers a silvery lavender. There is a white variety of much charm. An average soil and all possible sun are its simple wants. Propagate by seeds or cuttings.

P. SIX HILLS. A hybrid, with the foregoing as a possible parent, and a very good and pleasant thing it is, with no fads so long as it gets a reasonably free soil and a place in the sun. A widespread bush of only about 6–8 in. with grey-green leaves and a long succession of pale mauve trumpets.

PHLOX ADSURGENS. A recent introduction, the good wine of the phlox household. Trailing about with reddish stems beset with oval leaves, heads of blossom appear in May to continue more or less the whole season. These flowers vary a trifle, but normally the petals are a deliciously soft rosy cream with a pink line at the centre of each. A hardy, good-tempered plant for a cool bed of vegetable soil, lightly shaded. Early summer cuttings strike readily (see p. 62).

P. AMŒNA. A beautiful species not nearly well enough known. It is a broad-leaved, widely clumpy plant of about 8 in. yielding in early summer ample clusters of large, well-rounded flowers in a warm, rich pink. Hardy and content in any decent loam rendered free with leafmould and grit (see p. 66).

P. CAMLA. The prince of mossies. A superb hybrid, looser and taller in growth than other mossies and bearing bold heads of 1-in. well-formed flowers in a lovely shade of soft flesh-pink. It does well in an ordinary sandy loam with sharp drainage. Can be raised from cuttings, but not easily.

P. STELLARIA G. F. WILSON. This variety must take a high place, if not the highest, in the free-growing stellaria section. It is more lax in manner, taller and more ambitious than the average subulata and very lovely, when its tousled rug is lit with the clear, almost electric blue of its bonny flowers.

P. SUBULATA. A name covering a score of mat-forming phloxes, and all of them are happy, care-free plants for a sunny spot in any rock-garden soil. Perhaps the soft pink Vivid and rosier Daisy Hill (see p. 56) hold the fort in their own colours, but the blue-lilac Fairy, the whites May Snow and nivalis, and the crimson-magenta Sensation must be included in a selection. All these phloxes, like the last-named, will be quite satisfied with the usual catering provided by the everyday rock garden.

PHYLLODOCE EMPETRIFORMIS. No one who has a lime-free soil can overlook this delightful heath plant. Its semi-prostrate branches are furnished with bristly, linear, leaves, and from early summer it bears at their tips in erect clusters urn-shaped flowers in a clear flesh-pink. It will do in a flat bed of sandy loam enriched with vegetable compost, leafmould or peat and give long and care-free service.

P. NIPPONICA. From Japan comes this pleasant little bush of 6 in. or more. Its fine heath-like leaves are dark green and it breaks out in summer with a galaxy of stumpy but clear-cut bells, pure white with an occasional flush of rose. Give it the same conditions as the last-mentioned, but a closer-up position, and it will be an abiding joy. Can be raised from seed which ripens freely.

POLEMONIUM REPTANS. The best of the polemoniums are fastidious and nostalgic, the tallest are border plants, but P. reptans is suitable for rock gardens and it is singularly beautiful. It raises above its tuft of finely feathered leafage 9-in. stems bearing nodding wide-mouthed bells in an entrancing blue of luminous clarity. A tolerably cool but well-drained soil. Increase by division of the rhizomes.

POLYGALA CALCAREA. Of all milkworts this downland native deserves the place of honour among rock plants. Its evergreen mat, eventually covering a foot, is in May and June massed with short flower spikes of a most brilliant sapphire-blue. A limestone plant that does quite well in acid soil. A light, free medium, well drained and in full sun, is desirable. Very simply propagated by division.

P. CHAMÆBUXUS. A valuable alpine shrublet for the rougher parts of the rock garden. It seldom exceeds 8 in. but spreads by underground runners. The box-like leaves are ever-green, the pea-flowers yellow and ivory, but better than the type is P. C. purpurea, in which the blooms are larger and they have pink standard petals and a yellow keel. This latter is rarely out of flower the year round. Will prosper in any free soil in sun or shade.

P. VAYREDÆ. Evidently a geographical form of the above, but a smaller, neater creeping bushling of no less merit. The dark green leaves are narrower than in chamæbuxus and the more slenderly built blossoms flaunt a vivid rosy-magenta. As simple in its wants as the other; likes rather more sun. Both take a season or two to become established. They resent disturbance.

POLYGONUM AFFINE. One of the few knot-grasses permissible in the rock garden, and it is only suggested for the wilder parts. There, planted in a group, the soil being no more than moderately good, its spikes of rosy flowers will be followed by the rich orange, flame and red of its autumn leafage which persists into winter. For this latter alone it deserves a place.

POTENTILLA FRUTICOSA. This section of the shrubby cinquefoils contains a number of first-rate rock plants, all of them of an accommodating nature, ready to thrive and flower the greater part of the season in a medium to light soil; all need sun and can be increased by detaching rooted suckers or by cuttings. The following are a few of the choicest:

P. F. ARBUSCULA, a lax, semi-trailing shrub of 2 ft. or so with long slender branches, green leaves and 1½-in. flowers of the familiar rose pattern of the rest in a rich butter-yellow; BEESIANA, a shapely, erect and compact bush of about 18 in. The foliage is a silvered green, and yellow flowers like buttercups are borne from late May to November; FARRERI, a slender shrub of various forms, erect and prostrate, with deeply cut small green leaves and richly golden flowers over a long period. There is a pretty white form of this, a twiggy mound of 2 ft.; MANDSCHURICA is a more or less procumbent form covering eventually 2–3 sq. ft. with a height of 1 ft. At its best in early summer it maintains a succession of its shapely white flowers until autumn. An excellent rock shrub; PYRENAICA, also known as prostrata, is inclined to be flat growing but will mound up to a foot. Its leaves are grass-green and the flowers, borne all summer, are a rich, warm yellow.

P. NEPALENSIS WILLMOTTIÆ. A pocket edition of the much taller nepalensis (formosa) and an admirable rock plant. It presents a 4–5-in. tuft of its wild-strawberry leaves, and above these sprays of cherry-crimson flowers with a dark eye and freckling of golden anthers. It does in any sort of soil that is not cold and heavy and is seldom out of flower, even in winter often showing an odd bloom. May be raised from seed or increased by careful division.

P. RUPESTRIS. A stately plant of 12–18 in. and a rare native. Its erect stems of amber-green rise from a leafy base and terminate in heads of 1-in. flowers suggesting small white roses. A herb of quality and one that will carry on for years in a really dry spot. There is a wee Corsican form called P. r. pygmæ which does not get above 2–3 in., but its white flowers are comparatively large. Just the thing for a stone trough.

P. TONGUEI. A most comely little cinquefoil in the style of Miss Willmott's. Though smaller in leaf and growth the flowers are nearly 1 in. across and a rosy apricot with a crimson spot at the base of each petal. It is permanent and cheerful in a gritty loam.

P. VERNA. For this low-lying herb and its miniature, nana, we would always find a place, for both are prodigal in their output of golden, cup-shaped blossoms and their wants are few. Plenty of openness, a root run of soil too meagre for most plants and they will live long and cheerfully.

PRIMULA AURICULA. Parent of innumerable garden varieties and one of the oldest plants in cultivation, the typical auricula of the Alps must be given quarter in every rock garden. And it is a lovely plant, mealy of leaf and with heads of richly fragrant golden-yellow blossoms. It likes to be tucked into a bed of fibrous loam and old mortar between two boulders where it will not be parched. For some of its variously coloured offspring see P. pubescens.

P. EDGEWORTHII. Though a novelty and not too trustworthy under general treatment, this beautiful primula—a relative of P. Winteri—is well worth noting by the careful cultivator who can give it a place at the base of a wall or boulder, facing north or east. Its leaves, strap-shaped and pale green, make a clump of about 4 in., and during most of the winter, and early spring in particular, it produces a wealth of finely cut blossoms which, in its best form, are a vividly clear rose with a white eye. A gritty bed of leafmould and sandy loam should suit it (see p. 51).

P. FARINOSA and FRONDOSA. The bird-eye primrose is one of the most charming of British plants. Though fond of swampy places in the wild it will do in a mixture of honest loam and leafmould, with sun, if not allowed to get too dry. From its rosette of leaves it puts up 4–6-in. stems bearing heads of golden-eyed rosy flowers, but there are several colour forms in cultivation. It is advisable to lift and divide oldish clumps, preferably in early spring. P. frondosa is closely related and differs mainly in its leaves being powdered on both sides and the flower stems are shorter. Also it is more reliably perennial than its ally and less dependent on periodical division.

P. INVOLUCRATA. A delightful primula for a sunny bed in a moist soil, producing from a rosette of glossy green, spoon-shaped leaves, 10–12-in. stems topped by umbels of pure white, sweet-scented flowers in May. This elegant and refined plant, readily raised from seed, should always be grouped.

P. JULIÆ. One of the most valuable introductions of recent years, this little primrose from the Caucasus, with small and crinkly purple-stained leaves and flowers of rich burgundy, is ready to respond to any treatment. Whether it is grown singly or in groups it and its numerous varieties will never fail to give a gay return in colour in spring and during most of summer. Occasional division is helpful but not essential. A selection of Julianas should include Pam and Vulcan, both very petite and darkly magenta-crimson; Gloria, larger in much the same intense colour; Merton Hybrid, orange and crimson-red; the orange-red E. R. Janes; and one or other of the whites.

P. MARGINATA. The ideal rock primrose, this familiar plant, its toothed leaves silver edged and with trusses of blue-lavender, fragrant blossoms, will do anywhere, in sun or shade, in any soil, limy or otherwise. It will plod along year after year, even under neglect.

P. M. LINDA POPE. Doubtless the most charming of the marginatas and a lovely thing, its broad leaves and scapes white-powdered and, on 3-in. stems, small heads of perfectly formed flowers in a cool lavender. May be grown outdoors in a bed of gritty leafmould and sandy loam with a good top-dressing of stone chips. Light shade is desirable (see p. 67).

P. PUBESCENS. A group name covering hybrids of P. Auricula and allied alpine species. These include the crimson Faldonside; The General in brick-red; the white, alba; Ruby, as described by its name; and Mrs. J. H. Wilson, perhaps the best of all, with rosy-mauve scented flowers. These have the look of a small auricula and respond to similar treatment. Especially good for stone troughs. Increased by careful division.

P. ROSEA. An early introduction and one whose place in a cool soil, by the pool side or in shallow water has never been challenged. A March–April bloomer, raising above its leafless clumps 8-in. stems crowned with a cluster of rosy-carmine yellow-eyed blossoms. Colour forms, even more brilliant than the type, include Visser de Geer (large-flowered) and Brockhurst. Division or seed; often yields self-sown seedlings.

P. SECUNDIFLORA. Another lovely primula for a moist, vegetable soil. From a tuft of long narrow leaves ascend 12–18-in. stems carrying heads of pendulous bells in a rich wine-red set-off with mealy calyces, striped black and white. A primula of quality and quite amenable to garden life. Seed.

P. SERTULUM. An engaging little mite after the style of farinosa, but instead of staying put it issues runners like a strawberry at the ends of which baby sertulums arise. Each rosette of leaves presents a cluster of rose-lilac flowers on 4-in. stems. Not at all uneasy in a free soil with leafmould, and it does its own propagation as described.

P. WINTERI. One of the loveliest of all primulas and a plant that is much less fastidious than it is believed to be. It can be grown well under the lee of a north or east wall or shelving rock, in a shady wall crevice or quite in the open where winter rain is not excessive. It makes a hearty rosette of broad, pea-green, prettily puckered leaves, white-mealed, and from November to April brightens the winter with its beautiful cool lavender-blue, yellow-centred blossoms. Worthy of it is the chaste pure white form. A dryish winter, moisture in summer and a freely drained bed of sandy loam, leafmould and grit will generally succeed. Seed and division (see p. 38).

RAMONDIA PYRENAICA. Choicest of all plants for a shady rock crevice, this charming plant is at once known by its deep green, flat rosette of broad, mat-surfaced leaves, from beneath which 4-in. flower stems protrude in late spring. These bear a small head of large violet-blue blossoms with an orange eye, and there are white, pink and other varieties. Stuff the crevice with a mixture of old peat, leafmould and loam and ramondia will respond with a will. Increased by seed or leaf cuttings.

RANUNCULUS AMPLEXICAULIS. Doubtless the most attractive and satisfactory of rock-garden buttercups. A clumpy plant of 9 in. or so with bluish leaves and, come June, several branched stems yielding white buttercups which in the wild show departures in blush and pink. Good for a low-down bed of rich loam, backed if you will by the steely-leaved, golden-flowered R. gramineus, 9–12 in., which blooms all summer.

RAOULIA AUSTRALIS. For a light soil or scree in an open spot this tiny creeper will cover a wide space with a shingle of silver which is dusted with a peppering of yellow flowers in summer. An equally small but more vigorous relation is the emerald-green glabra with rather less minute silver and yellow blossoms. And there is an intermediate species, the grey-green subsericea.

RHODODENDRON. This great family is beyond the scope of these pages, but the dwarfs are such admirable rock shrubs that a few must be noted. One of the best and smallest is R. radicans, a prostrate creeper with purple flowers; keleticum is rather larger in much the same style; impeditum, a close-set, deep green mound with violet blossoms, is excellent; and Hanceanum nanum (see p. 66), with yellow trusses, is a perfect example of the close, dome-shaped style that is so suitable. R. intricatum in a lovely lavender, chryseum a good yellow and Forrest's racemosum in flesh-pink are not to be overlooked. And there are hosts of others, all neat little bushes that will give no trouble in a lime-free loam, with humus, and blossom luxuriantly every spring and often again in autumn. Most of them can very quickly be raised from seed or increased by cuttings.

RHODOHYPOXIS BAURII. A queer little member of the Daffodil family. Its tufts of leaves are only 2 in. high, and the starry flowers, not much taller, are bright cherry-pink and borne from June onwards. Hardy and successful in a gravel-bed or scree. There is a good white form, platypetala, among others (see p. 58).

ROSA ROULETTII. The smallest of the fairy roses and a delightful oddity for a close-up ledge. It seldom exceeds 4–5 in. and bears double China roses all summer. Ordinary light soil; sun; may be produced from cuttings.

ROSCŒA ALPINA. One of the aristocrats of rock gardens, this curiosity of about 6 in. produces a close tuft of broad, deep green leaves, and among them in full summer appear the orchid-like flowers. These are usually a bluish-lavender, or violet, and large for the size of the plant. This and the rather more robust R. Humeana, with rich wine-purple flowers, are the pick of the race for rock gardens, and they do well in a deep, freely drained, cool loam, not too dry. Seed (see p. 65).

RUBUS ARCTICUS. A dainty wee bramble of only 3 in., most attractive rambling about by its underground branches among such shrubs as rhododendrons, and relishes similar conditions. The flowers are rose-pink, the size of a sixpence. Yellow fruits are sometimes produced.

SANGUINARIA CANADENSIS. The Canadian blood-root is a very lovely plant starting in spring with a dove-grey leaf scroll from which emerges a beautiful pure white anemone flower with many slender rays. This for a partly shaded pocket of rich, moist vegetable loam. Established clumps should not be disturbed. As the large scalloped leaves die down early, the plant must be permanently labelled lest it be accidentally dug up. May be propagated by seed. There is a double variety, still rare, but a very beautiful plant.

SAPONARIA OCYMOIDES. The soapworts offer this estimable species for rock gardens, and it is a hearty thing when, trailing down a slope, it flushes into bright pink in summer. The variety splendens is richer in colour, and there is a pure white which deserves wider appreciation. Any soil will satisfy these easy-going things. They come readily from seed, special varieties from cuttings.

SAXIFRAGA. Of the roaming herds of the saxifrages we propose to deal only with four sections—the Mossy, the Silver, Cushion and Engleria—and that very briefly, merely mentioning a few favourites of personality and charm that are of general usefulness.

THE MOSSIES. These weave dense mats and mounds of fresh green indented leaves and delight in a fairly cool soil and position. They can all be increased by division and may need periodical replanting owing to their foliage growing patchy. The closest and most permanent are the moschatas, containing such excellent kinds as the rose-crimson Stormonth's Variety; the pale pink Wild Rose; and wee purpurea, a green cushion bristling with rosy-headed pins. Other distinguished mossies are the white, James Bremner (see p. 63); sanguinea superba and Sir D. Haig, deep velvety crimson; Wallacei, a fine old white; Pompadour, richest crimson; Triumph, a non-fading deep red.

THE SILVERS OR ENCRUSTEDS. The chief features here are rosettes of narrow leathery leaves, usually embroidered with limy encrustations. These may be single or in colonies, and the flowers, most commonly white, are borne on stems soaring to 2 ft. or more. An easy-going tribe, ready to make good in a poor, stony slope, in a rock chink or wall, and they do not insist on full sun. In a short list I would not omit the 9-in. aizoons, lutea and rosea, yellow and pink respectively; cochlearis, a silvery conglomerate of small rosettes and 3-in. red-stemmed sprays of white; Kathleen Pinsent, a lovely pink; longifolia, including the sensational Tumbling Waters.

THE CUSHIONS (KABSCHIA). An important and numerous group of high alpines, dwarf and cushiony in habit and for the most part limy-leaved. Not difficult in scree, on slopes of very gritty soil, in stone troughs or rocky fissures, with a generous ration of sun. A selection should include the early apiculata, both yellow and white, Arco-Valley, a dainty atom in cherry-pink. The wonderful Burserianas are too early for successful outdoor culture generally, but cæsia is a pleasing little white crevice lover, and the yellow Faldonside, though early, is too good to be omitted. Irvingi with pink flowers, or the rather superior Jenkinsii, are also among the chosen; the excellent Myra can be risked with a pane of glass to protect its cherry-red blossoms; and the yellow Paulinæ is most reliable.

THE ENGLERIAS. Almost essentially alpine house plants, but many can be made at home in scree or stone troughs, filled with a gritty compost. The pride of the race is S. Grisebachii, and with the Wisley Variety of this remarkable species we shall here be content. Perhaps the most beautiful of all rock saxifrages, this consists of beehive rosettes of closely overlapping steely blue leaves, each about 2 in. across. In spring the apex of the beehive puts forth a 6-in. crozier, rich in ruby velvet and bearing pink flowers which are quite eclipsed by the splendour of the stem. This striking plant is quite permanent in a stone trough or crevice and may be increased by detaching offsets. Indeed, practically all the foregoing can be propagated by this simple means, but it may be necessary to pot and nurse the portions in a frame until well rooted.

S. GRANULATA. A delightful native producing from a mat of bright green, lobed leaves 9-in. stately stems hung at the summit with finely drawn white bells. There is a double variety, only recommended on account of it lasting longer in bloom. A charming plant for a low-down, moistish bed of ordinary soil. Easily increased by division of the pill-like tubers.

S. UMBROSA. Quite the best of this group is Elliott's Variety. Virtually a " London Pride " in miniature with small and huddled green rosettes, soon making a wide mat, and 4-6-in. red-stemmed sprays with a glitter of ruby-pink flowers. A very choice little plant for a coolish place and not too rich a soil. It loves to creep over a low mossy boulder, and there it is singularly enchanting. One of the easiest and most adaptable plants alive.

SCABIOSA GRAMINIFOLIA. A wisp of grassy leaves, soft and grey with silky hairs, and over it in summer large flowers of the usual scabious mode in a gentle lavender with a hint of french-grey and rose. An ideal and very lovely plant for a dry, hot wall or rock cleft. Late summer cuttings.

SEDUM. Though most of them possess the virtue of putting up with any sort of a life, it is an error, oft committed, to imagine that all stonecrops appreciate life in a waterless desert. S. spathulifolium purpureum, with flat, mealy dove-grey rosettes, crimson in winter, likes a good loam so long as it is free and covered with anti-splash chips. This is one of the best, but we like ternatum also, with bird's-claw inflorescences glittering with crystal stars, and it also enjoys similar conditions. S. oregonum, with fat plum-coloured leaves, will blush crimson with starvation wrought by drought, and it then looks well with its golden flower-heads. The old S. spurium is not to be hastily turned down, for it can be showy enough in a decent soil, given one of its better forms, splendens, or the new Schorbusser Blut, which approaches carmine. Then for a really moist spot there is the beautiful S. pulchellum, a harmonious blend of frosty-emerald foliage and broad heads of rosy-lilac.

SEMPERVIVUM. The house-leeks, on the other hand, have a passion for the most sun-baked and arid crevices in wall or boulder, and very useful they are for plastering such fissures with their variously coloured rosettes. There are teeming hordes of them, but few have quite the charm of the cobwebbed varieties of S. arachnoideum (see p. 53), and few are more easily grown. The rosettes of this species vary very greatly in size and colour, all are beautiful, with their gossamer strands stretched from leaf-tip to leaf-tip, and their brick-red flowers are distinctly ornamental.

SILENE SCHAFTA. S. alpestris is a good white of this genus with a winning and easy way, but we would award the honours here to schafta because it is so welcome in the late season when colour is on the wane. A bunchy plant of 4 in., it will carry a mass of rosy-claret blossoms for many weeks and demand nothing in the way of attention, being happy in a well-drained loam with sun. Seed.

SPIRÆA DIGITATA NANA. A bright and useful little plant of only about 9 in., but crested with a foam of blossom in the raspberry-pink dye of the splendid S. palmata, of which it suggests a miniature. Quite amenable in any not too dry soil, and it flowers throughout the later summer.

SYNTHYRIS RENIFORMIS. This shade-loving American produces a bushy tuft of kidney-shaped leaves and erect 6-in. trusses of blossom in a rich sapphire-blue. With some leafmould and a rather moist soil it can be expected to live long and heartily.

TEUCRIUM PYRENAICUM. Not a showy plant but always appealing in its flattish growth, hairy leaves and coronets of little hooded blossoms (midsummer), which are a creamy ivory with a touch of lilac. A warm, free soil with full sun. Division or seed.

THYMUS HERBA-BARONA. The Seedcake Thyme is a creeper after the style of T. Serpyllum but darker in foliage, looser and more wiry. Grown mainly for the fragrance of caraway which its leaves emit. Warm ledge of thin soil.

T. MEMBRANACEUS. A thrilling 4–6-in. bushling with scented foliage and large white-bracted flowers unlike those of any other. Light gravelly soil; sun. A good stone-trough plant.

T. NITIDUS. One of the best of rock-garden shrubs, making a clumpy bush of 12 in. with grey aromatic leaves and a profusion of lilac blossoms. Any lean, stony soil; full sun. Selected forms best raised from cuttings (see p. 64).

T. SERPYLLUM. Our sweet moorland thyme makes a delightful sward of its changeful greens and includes many beautiful varieties. Notable among these are the crimson coccineus majus ; the white with grass-green foliage ; Annie Hall, flesh-pink ; and Pink Chintz, later than most and a clear pink. All summer bloomers and ground-hugging creepers. A meagre soil; all possible sun.

TIARELLA CORDIFOLIA. A creeping woodlander for any coolish spot in the rock garden where it may enmesh a boulder with a network of its runners and prettily lobed leaves which turn a fine scarlet in autumn. Flower spikes of 6 in., fluffy and white, are raised in the later spring. Division.

VERONICA ARMENA. A procumbent species making a mat of finely cut, deep green leaves and bearing in June and after speedwell flowers in a rich blue. Hardy and permanent in a warm soil.

V. BIDWILLII. This is a wee New Zealander, a close mat of tangled stems, tiny rounded leaves and light 3-in. sprays of white flowers. A dainty for a choice place, but most of us find the larger V. B. Miss Willmott more tractable and lasting. Both need sharp drainage, a gritty root-run and sun.

V. CINEREA. Bushy, grey-white and about 6 in., this is a nice plant for a hot, sunny ledge. It is delicately lovely, with its pale, sky-blue flowers against its ashen foliage, and quite tolerably hardy.

V. GENTIANOIDES. From low tufts of leathery deep green leaves this raises 18-in. spires hung with starch-blue blossoms. A stately plant and a valuable one for imparting height to an otherwise flat planting. Any soil; division.

V. GUTHRIANA. Anyone who cannot satisfy saxatilis will be well content with this little 4-6-in. bushling with its sombre leafage and brilliant rich blue blossoms. A good-tempered thing anywhere and one that will propagate itself by self-sown seed.

V. SAXATILIS. Perhaps the loveliest speedwell of all and a rare native. A frail sub-shrubby species with small glossy leaves and very large brilliant blue blossoms with a ring of red at the centre. St. John's is a variety of great merit, nearer gentian-blue than the type. A gritty soil, or scree, with sun, for this treasure. Seed.

V. TEUCRIUM. Often known as V. rupestris, this is one of the most indispensable of all rock-garden speedwells. The type spreads spacious mats of green which bristle with 3-in. flower spikes in sapphire blue, rose or white, some outstanding forms being the rose-pink Mrs. Holt and Spode Blue, both about 4 in. Taller varieties of this group with a tufted growth and erect flower stems (6-12 in.) are Royal Blue, Shirley Blue, and the golden-leaved Trehane with sapphire spikes, a most striking variety. All divide easily and prosper in ordinary soil.

VIOLA BOSNIACA. This viola is almost unique in its bright rose-pink blossoms. It is easily raised from seed, but not long-lived, and in most gardens the very similar but larger Crimson King is more trustworthy. Light soil and sun.

V. CORNUTA. The old horned violet is one of the most useful of the family, a robust and easy-going plant that will do under any conditions and all summer maintain a succession of its large blue, purple or white flowers (see p. 68). Many varieties and hybrids, including the sensational Jersey Gem and a diminutive called Dainty, a charming midget and great bloomer.

V. GRACILIS. Perhaps the most winsome and elegant of all alpine violas, with narrow leaves and quantities of elfin blossoms in a royal purple, rich and glossy. There is an outsize called major, a very fine thing, and numerous hybrids. These latter are a sweet-tempered most flowery race and of the utmost value, blooming profusely nearly all the season and prospering in any reasonable soil. They include the almost black Black Knight; Clarence Elliott, white; Golden Wave, rich yellow; Lady Crisp, lavender-blue; and Moonlight, pale ivory-yellow.

LEWISIA TWEEDYI

Lewisias are not for everybody, but some are too fascinating to resist, and one of these is L. Tweedyi. It has a flattish rosette of fleshy leaves and 2-in. flowers of a most alluring shade of apricot. A sandy loam enriched with leafmould and mixed with small granite chips, with perfect drainage, the bed being on a sunny slope, seems to be agreeable to the beauty. But a pane of glass tilted over it in winter is a wise precaution. Most of the lewisias can be raised from seed, and seedlings may be tried in westerly wall crevices.

PRIMULA WINTERI

CAMPANULA JENKINSÆ

CROCUS TOMASINIANUS

A February to May crocus of unsurpassed loveliness and one of the most reliable. Its slender "wine-glasses," french-grey in the bud, open to a silvery violet with scarlet stigmata, and they are deliciously fragrant. Refined to proportions appropriate to the most exclusive of small rock gardens, this crocus is also light in leafage. It will naturalise under almost any conditions. There are colour variations, including some good purples.

ARMERIA MARITIMA

As on the sea-cliffs, so among alpines, the familiar thrift proves itself an ideal rock plant. Content with a mere stony fissure, but responding to better treatment, it crowns its grassy mops in the later spring with drumsticks of varying size in colours that range from white through blush to pink, lilac and rosy-crimson (vars. Laucheana and Vindictive). May be propagated by division or seed. A sun lover. Limestone or granite.

ANEMONE HEPATICA

For a shady crevice there is no better plant than this. It carries in succession from February to May 1-in. flowers in many shades of blue, lavender and rose with a freckling of white anthers. There are doubles of most varieties, a good white, and closely akin is A. angulosa with larger blue blossoms and evergreen leaves. All these thrive in a cool loam with leaf-mould and grit, and they are often as happy on the flat as in a rocky cleft. They dislike disturbance.

CAMPANULA HAYLODGENSIS PLENA

MUSCARI BOTRYOIDES ALBUM

DRYAS OCTOPETALA

A creeping alpine shrublet with crinkled evergreen oak-like leaves, this delightful plant should be given a square yard of sloping bed with a few low rocks for it to mound over. Creamy-white flowers, like little dog-roses, are borne in spring and summer, and these are succeeded by seed-heads of tousled silk. Any average soil, not too heavy, and full sun. There is a miniature form, minor, and the creamy-yellow hybrid, Sundermannii.

CORNUS CANADENSIS

This little creeping dogwood of North American woods makes a delightful feature for a shady side of the rock garden. The rosette of broad green leaves which tops each 4-in. stem is centred during late spring and summer with the gleaming white bracts which surround the inconspicuous flowers. The foliage develops rich autumn tints, and after the flowers come (sometimes) red berries. Light but cool lime-free soil with humus is what it enjoys. Increase by division.

CYCLAMEN NEAPOLITANUM

For a lightly shaded corner this is an invaluable plant, for it produces its jaunty rosy shuttle-cocks in autumn, and all winter we have the beautiful ivy-like leaves in diversions of green with pencillings and frostings of silver. Equally charming is the white variety, and these only ask a bed of humous soil, shallow planting and to be left alone and they will live for ever, slowly colonising with their seed-raised offspring.

ASTER MARJORIE

CYCLAMEN COUM ALBUM

AZALEA HINOMAYO

DAPHNE CNEORUM EXIMIA

47

ASTER ALPINUS

This glory of many an alpine pasture is a first-rate rock plant, easy, hardy and long-lived. Above a woody clump, perhaps a foot across, it raises 6-in. stems each bearing (May) a single golden-eyed daisy, often with doubled rays, which may be any colour from white to slaty lavender, pink, blue-purple and deepest violet. Should be lifted and divided about every third year. Any average lightish soil, not too dry; full sun.

AETHiONEMA WARLEY ROSE

One of the loveliest of the alpine candytufts and an indispensable rock-garden plant, making a little bush of about 6 in. with a spread of 12 in. The evergreen leaves are steely blue, and over them in spring is raised a throng of flower-spikes in a brilliant rose-pink. An easy plant in a deep but gritty, or stony, soil with full sun. Cannot be raised from seed, for it is a sterile hybrid, but it comes readily from August cuttings.

DIANTHUS BOYDII

CAMPANULA CARPATICA

GENTIANA SINO-ORNATA

PRIMULA EDGEWORTHII

ANEMONE APENNINA

The bluest and best of all blue anemones, this charming windflower is at home in almost any conditions, but it enjoys a moderately cool soil with humus and light shade. Rather taller than our own wood anemone, it is equally ready to colonise and never fails to yield in abundance (March to May) its many-rayed, gentian-blue flowers. There are pink, rose and white varieties. It moves best in summer just after dying down.

JUNIPERUS COMMUNIS COMPRESSA AND SEMPERVIVUM ARACHNOIDEUM

This little juniper is the perfection of rock-garden conifers. It raises an erect close-set cone of minute blue-green foliage and never outgrows its position. The specimen shown above is 10 in. high and ten years old and will possibly attain 20 in. or more. It occupies the margin of a rocky colony of house-leeks. A rather meagre soil is desirable, with a commanding position among the smaller plants with full sun.

ARMERIA MARITIMA VINDICTIVE

LEUCOJUM VERNUM CARPATHICUM

PENTSTEMON NEWBERRYI RUPICOLA

Most precious of all the lesser pentstemons, this little flat-growing plant, with its gnarled branches, small blue-green leathery leaves and huge trumpets of dazzling ruby-crimson, is beyond price. It is, moreover, hardy and prevailing, the ideal thing for a stony slope or rock crevice, limestone or granite, in full sun. Spring is its high season. Can be raised from seed or soft cuttings taken after flowering. Known also as P. Davidsoni and Menziesii Douglasii.

PHLOX SUBULATA DAISY HILL

CYTISUS LEUCANTHUS

GENTIANA SEPTEMFIDA

A gentian without fad or foible in any decent loam, limy or acid, yet one of the finest of the family. It presents a tuft of more or less procumbent, 9–12-in. growths terminating in a cluster of large upturned bells, clear blue with a fringed mouth and silvery speckled throat. Flowers from midsummer onwards. Needs no special culture but resents disturbance. Likes full sun. There are several forms of this gentian, cordifolia and the smaller lagodechiana being among the most distinct.

ALYSSUM SAXATILE VAR. CITRINUM

RHODOHYPOXIS BAURII

ARENARIA MONTANA

A robust and very beautiful trailer, eventually covering several square feet. From May onwards it yields a profusion of milk-white blooms fully 1 in. across. Though normally only 4–6 in. high, it will clamber into any neighbourly shrub and envelop it to the height of a couple of feet. Increase by seed or rooted portions. It may spread naturally by seeding but is never a menace.

CASSIOPE SELAGINOIDES

In many respects the best of a somewhat fastidious race, this choice little shrub will appeal to every connoisseur who has a partly shaded lime-free bed of leafmould, old peat and grit to offer it. Its whipcord branches, vivid green and some 8 in. high, carry in spring finely wrought milk-white bells, and of these a succession is maintained until full summer.

DABOËCIA CANTABRICA

The Connemara Heath, an excellent shrub for the bolder parts of the rock garden, makes about 18 in. with a spread of 2–4 ft. Typically, the large egg-shaped bells (full summer) are rosy-mauve, but there is a good crimson-purple and others, including an excellent white. This last will flower from late spring to autumn and it comes true from seed. The very large-flowered globosa, clear rose-lilac, is a fine variety. Light lime-free soil containing some form of humus and full sun.

DIANTHUS LA BOURBRILLE

PHLOX ADSURGENS

SAXIFRAGA JAMES BREMNER

Among the hosts of mossy saxifrages, this variety stands out as a white of superlative merit. It bears on 8-in. stems milk-white blossoms of waxen texture the size of a florin. Like other mossies, it indicates its appreciation of somewhat cool conditions by yielding finer blossoms, remaining longer in flower and by maintaining the verdure of its close mats of green foliage which are so charming always, even in mid-winter.

OXALIS ADENOPHYLLA

THYMUS NITIDUS

ROSCŒA ALPINA

ANACYCLUS DEPRESSUS

PHLOX AMŒNA

RHODODENDRON HANCEANUM NANUM

DAPHNE PETRÆA

PRIMULA LINDA POPE

VIOLA CORNUTA ALBA

GERANIUM LANCASTRIENSE

FLOWERING TREES
AND SHRUBS

URING their long story our gardens have seen many changes, but none had so radical an influence as the adoption of the informal, more natural lay-out in place of the formal of mid-Victorian days. This break-away from a style that was as rigid in its policy as it was in effect, this abandonment of the geometrical for the lines of the landscape artist, gave the shrub its opportunity. For while in the prim bedding schemes of earlier days it had no place, here in this new conception of gardening it at once took a leading part. Shrubs became its key features, the very fabric of its making.

This drift from the formal into a system in which shrubs would occupy a prominent position was, however, something more than a mere swing of fashion's pendulum. It began to take definite shape when costs of maintenance were giving garden owners increasing anxiety, and it soon became manifest that relief from this burden could be acquired by shrub culture. Moreover, we were not long in realising that a garden in which shrubs were a dominant feature might provide as much beauty, pleasure and interest as any other, perhaps more, and these at all seasons. It happened, further, that just about the time this transfiguration of our gardens was taking place, our growing appreciation of shrubs derived immense stimulus from those introductions of new species from America, Asia, the Antipodes and elsewhere, which, commencing in limited numbers at rare intervals, soon developed into a steady stream of novelties which has grown largely in volume and splendour until the present day.

So shrub culture came into its own. It was hailed by the big man as well as by the small as a heaven-sent refuge from the tedium and expense of the gardening that preceded it. And if it were the owner of wide acres who was the first to grasp its immense possibilities, there is not the slightest doubt but that the opening of our large gardens to the public under the Queen's Institute of District Nursing Association has more recently had a profound influence in demonstrating to the rank and file the beauty of shrubs, their place in the garden and the enormous saving of labour their use implies.

It might be urged that the price of shrubs is relatively high. This may be, but against that one has the satisfaction of knowing that the first cost is the only one, and, after all, many a good variety can be secured for a shilling or two. But if our gardens as well as our resources are to derive the fullest benefit from this departure, without which economy will be a deception, it follows that we must neither be parsimonious in our initial investments nor at fault in our practical treatment, which latter involves the deriving of the fullest possible returns for our outlay both as regards the shrubs individually and their influence upon the garden. That is to say, we must concentrate on shrubs of proved merit and so treat them that they will yield their utmost value as garden amenities. And let it be re-emphasised that it always pays to go in for the best, not necessarily the newest, rarest and most expensive—this is often a delusion—but those of tried garden value and distinguished

E

ornamental status. The days of the old-fashioned "shrubbery," that meaningless, often wasteful muddle, are gone for ever. The era of the individual shrub, regarded both as an isolated specimen or as a group unit, has arrived, bringing with it a garden change that is supremely satisfying and that with a substantial saving in upkeep and release from worry.

In the pages following we have compiled a list of shrubs most of which have won general esteem. Even so, such a selection, necessarily much abbreviated, will not satisfy everybody. No claim of the sort has been attempted, for tastes differ widely and everyone must discover for himself what will do well in his soil and conditions. And this latter is an important point, for if we are to avoid trouble and expense and realise the fullest results, it is essential to choose plants to suit the place they are to occupy rather than attempt to grow them under antagonistic conditions. That, at all events, is a safe general rule. The specialist, if he will, may do otherwise and, being what he is, enjoy the fruits of his labour.

On the arrangement of shrubs little of a definite nature can be said here for the obvious reason that gardens vary so enormously in size, aspect, contour and other factors. A border in which the shrubs are so widely spread that they afford room between them for lilies, spring bulbs or such herbaceous plants as peonies, commends itself to many gardens. Then, where space allows, there is nothing more beautiful than the glade principle, in which shrubs occupy both sides, as in the border, with a backing of thinly disposed trees for such shade-lovers as rhododendrons and azaleas, while in between is a sweep of turf, best of settings for most flowering shrubs. Woodland also affords many opportunities for indulgence in shrubs where the trees are wide apart and their lower branches cut away, and "specimen" trees, usually placed in the lawn or in some other commanding position, must also be sympathetically considered. Then there are great possibilities in the growing of shrubs in groups, these being of a naturally gregarious nature, like many of the lesser rhododendrons, heaths and brooms. Given a suitable site, preferably a gentle slope to the front, some very lovely effects can be acquired thus, and with most of the colony shrubs mentioned, and many others, such a planting will become entirely carefree.

The permanency of shrubs being from a practical point of view one of their most valuable attributes, ample room for their development must be provided. But this does not imply that a wide earth space between each is inevitable. The chosen individuals may be interplanted with less permanent things, as suggested, until such time as they in their maturity all but touch one another. Indeed, in grouping such plants as heaths, rhododendrons and azaleas, which move easily with a ball of soil, the spacing may be so close that they will join up in a season or two, when the temporary individuals may be gradually thinned out until only those correctly spaced to remain are left in possession.

There is now such a vast choice in flowering shrubs and trees that the owner of even a moderate-sized garden is able so to make his selection that he will have something in bloom from January to December. Some of us can remember the days when there was little else in winter-flowering shrubs beyond the old laurestinus. But since that time the "dead months" have become increasingly alive with the witch-hazels, viburnums, winter cherry and massed colours of the heaths, to say nothing of rhododendrons that begin early in February and continue without a break until the main flourish of the spring. So it is in the days of late summer and autumn which were once comparatively wanting in flowering shrubs. The beautiful eucryphias alone are now sufficient to adorn that season with incomparable grace, and so the entire year to the shrub grower of enterprise is a round of loveliness and interest.

FLOWERING TREES AND SHRUBS

The economic side of shrub growing, as well as one's ultimate satisfaction, must depend considerably upon the preparation of the soil, for unless a plant is healthy and content it will not give of its best, nor will we be immune from that anxiety we are planning to avoid. But soil preparation need not be any more laborious than is undertaken for any other class of plant. It may often be less, as in the planting of lawn trees or woodland shrubs. Where, however, it is intended to stock beds or borders it will pay and pay well thoroughly to trench the site. Soils differ, of course, in their needs, but a good twenty-inch bastard-trenching, plus the breaking up of the subsoil with a pick energetically wielded, will serve for an average medium. If the latter is thin and mean the more vegetable compost that can be worked into it the better it will be for most things, but we repeat that the owner who has to deal with such meagre ground will be wiser to focus his attention on brooms, heaths, cistuses and the like rather than attempt camellias and magnolias. The ground for shrubs should always be prepared some months before the planting season is due. For if the soil has not settled down by the time the shrubs are being put in, sinking is almost sure to occur, and this may have most detrimental results on the welfare of many subjects.

On the all-important matter of maintenance something must be said, for it is here, as we have stated, that the shrub wins over most plants. To put the matter briefly, a shrub or specimen tree properly planted and temporarily staked should need no further attention. As to pruning, this can practically be disposed of altogether with the majority of subjects. Evergreens, at all events, can, as a whole, be left entirely alone. Others, as indicated in the forthcoming pages, may need the removal of dead and worn-out branches at intervals, or the cutting back of flowering wood when blooming ceases. But although there is very little systematic pruning called for in dealing with shrubs in general, there are some folk, perhaps rather many, who make a fuss over it, and this is not only a waste of time that might be more wisely employed but it tends to rob many shrubs of their natural grace.

Transplanting may often be necessary, and the success of this operation, like that of original planting, depends a good deal upon the season chosen for the job. With deciduous shrubs we prefer to move (or plant) them as soon as the leaves go off, provided the soil is nice and moist, otherwise they are left until late February or March. Evergreens are more touchy—rhododendrons being an exception—and for most of these we think April, or even May, the safest time. Watering may on some soils have to be done during the first summer with these newly moved plants, but a considerable saving of this labour may be realised by placing over the roots a surface mulch of compost, preferably mixed with equal parts of moss-peat that has been well weathered. This mulching, in addition to being a means of conserving moisture, will be all that is needed in the way of feeding. For if the soil is tolerably good and the shrubs are given a fair start in life in a medium congenial to them, no further manuring or fertilising should be needed. They will go steadily ahead without demanding any more from us than a nod of approbation and prove to be an investment not only paying rich dividends year by year, but showing in their permanency and increase a steadily growing capital value in all that tends to foster the riper charms and fundamental principles of good gardening.

A SELECTION OF
FLOWERING TREES AND SHRUBS

ABELIA SCHUMANNII. The most reliable of a semi-hardy family, this is a good mixed border shrub of 4 ft. The arching branches are laden with tubular rose-lilac blossoms (May to September) with purple bracts retained after the flowers have fallen. Less hardy is the semi-scandent A. floribunda (see p. 98) with 2-in. rosy-red trumpets at midsummer. Needs a warm wall. A. grandiflora (4–5 ft.), with silver-pink flowers, is pleasing as a late bloomer. A light soil and full sun for all these. Cuttings or rooted off-sets.

ABUTILON VITIFOLIUM. A soft-wooded shrub of 12–20 ft. with downy vine-like leaves and, in early summer, large mallow flowers in various shades of blue, lavender, pale mauve and white. Fairly hardy, but should have a sheltering wall and free soil. Sun or part shade. Not long-lived. Fresh stock raised from seed; selected colour forms from cuttings. Another striking abutilon is A. magapotamicum, a slender wall plant bearing all summer pendulous egg-shaped blossoms, wine-red, yellow and maroon. Off-sets.

ÆSCULUS PARVIFLORA. The red horse-chestnuts are too large for the average garden, but this American is a widely spread but lowly shrub of only 5–6 ft. It has a handsome foliage, the erect pink and white " candles " are freely borne in August, and the shrub will give no trouble in any average loam. Increased by detaching rooted suckers. No pruning needed.

AMELANCHIER. A genus of shrubs and small trees notable for their spring blossom, beautiful young foliage and glorious autumn tints. They are hardy and easy in a moist, free soil. Best known is the snowy mespilus with white flowers in May, but still more attractive are the rosy-white A. asiatica, the white grandiflora with red-bronze leaves in spring and its pink-tinted variety, rubescens. A. levis is also very lovely, its white flowers among rosy-tinted leaves. Seed, layers or off-sets.

ARBUTUS UNEDO. One of the finest of all evergreens, and hardier than is generally supposed. Beautiful in winter with its panicles of urn-shaped white blossoms and in autumn when hung with strawberry-like crimson fruits. One of the few ericaceous shrubs that will tolerate lime. Another handsome species is A. Menziesii with larger leaves, bright glossy green, a rich terra-cotta bark and pyramidal panicles of white flowers followed by orange fruits. A good loamy soil, with humus and freely drained, will suit both of these. No pruning.

AZALEA (DECIDUOUS). Although azaleas are included in Rhododendron, they are dealt with separately here. Among the species a selection should include the rich rose-red Albrechtii; the late summer arborescens, rose and white; the splendid old yellow pontica and its fine form, Altaclarense; rosea, pink; the beautiful Vaseyi with clear rose-pink or white blossoms; and the wine-purple reticulata. The well-known azalea hybrids, with their

72

wonderful range of brilliant colours and delicious fragrance, are now too many to make even a brief choice possible. But in addition to the Ghents, mollis-sinensis and rustica fl. pl. groups I would suggest a careful survey of the occidentalis hybrids and the new Knap Hill strain as being worthy of special notice. From these and others let each one make a choice to satisfy his or her individual tastes.

AZALEA (EVERGREEN). In addition to those referred to in the Rock Garden pages, here are some azaleas of special merit : the pure white, fragrant A. ledifolia with a variety in rosy-lilac; balsaminæflora (rosæflora), low-growing, double salmon; amœna, magenta, ruby, white, pink; yodogawa, double blue-mauve ; and the summer-flowering macrostema, salmon-scarlet. Azaleas are well satisfied with a medium to light lime-free soil, with humus. Most of the evergreens enjoy sun, but light shade is desirable for the taller hybrids. Layers or cuttings.

AZARA MICROPHYLLA. A tall shrub or slender tree with graceful frond-like branches of small and glossy evergreen leaves and multitudes of minute yellow flowers in February, these emitting a delicious vanilla fragrance. Any light soil. Not very hardy.

BERBERIDOPSIS CORALLINA. An evergreen climber with glaucous-green, mahonia-like leaves and clusters of waxen blood-red blossoms in late summer. Fairly hardy on a wall. Prefers a N. or E. aspect. Non-limy soil, cool, moist and not wanting in humus—peat or leafy compost. Needs wires or some other support.

BERBERIS (FLOWERING EVERGREEN). The splendid B. Darwinii must take the lead here, for it is of inestimable garden worth, Flame, crimson and orange, and the rich golden-yellow, Gold, being selected forms. But there are many others, including dwarfs and hybrids. Among the latter, stenophylla, a large bush with long weeping branches gilded with orange blossoms, rivals Darwinii itself in splendour and general merit. Akin to stenophylla are several dwarfer shrubs of value, the best of which is the 4–6-ft. corallina with coral-red and orange flowers.

B. LINEARIFOLIA. This newcomer in its best forms (a variable plant) exceeds even Darwinii in size of blossom and the fiery brilliance of its orange, apricot and scarlet, and it is hardy. B. lologensis, a cross between this species and Darwinii, has also earned no little reputation in many gardens. Its very large flowers are apricot with a glowing orange interior.

BERBERIS (DECIDUOUS FRUITING). A selection of barberries for autumn fruit and leaf colour should include B. aggregata and Prattii; dictyophylla; polyantha; rubrostilla Wisley Variety ; Sieboldii; Thunbergii and Wilsonæ, all graceful bushes of 4–7 ft. The barberries in general do willingly in a medium loam, often on dry slopes, in sun or part shade. Most of them can be raised from cuttings, seed or rooted off-sets. Only pruning required consists of occasionally removing the older branches to make room for the new.

BUDDLEIA ALTERNIFOLIA. A hardy Chinese species of 10–15 ft. or more with a shower of slender weeping branches clustered at midsummer with fragrant mauve blossoms. Good loam; sun. Cuttings or basal suckers.

B. DAVIDII. The well-known purple buddleia, making graceful wands (after cutting hard back in spring) of 4–6 ft. Best varieties, amplissima and magnifica with large rich mauve and violet-purple panicles. Veitchii is earlier (June), and nanhoënsis a dwarf of 5–6 ft. with elegant branches tipped with mauve trusses. Also pink varieties (Pink Pearl, rosea, floribunda).

B. FALLOWIANA. A slender shrub of 6–8 ft. with grey-green leaves and late summer panicles of a soft smoke-blue. Also a variety with whiter leaves and white, orange-eyed flowers, very fragrant. Both to be cut back close to old wood in spring. Branches thus removed in this and above buddleias will root if shortened and laid in on a cool border.

B. GLOBOSA. A fine old buddleia with downy leaves and lax clusters of globular orange flowers, May to July. Prune lightly every alternate year soon as flowering ceases. Cuttings. This and all others are sun lovers but not fastidious in this respect or in regard to soil.

CALLUNA VULGARIS. The common ling offers many varieties of the highest garden value as late bloomers. One of the finest is the 3-ft. crimson Alportii. Hammondii is a tall white, and Mair's Variety, Serlei and the new double (alba fl. pl.) are also whites to be noted. In coloured doubles, the tall H. E. Beale, rose-pink, is pre-eminent, and County Wicklow and Camla Variety, both pinks, are charming plants. For others see Rock Garden section. A moderately moist, lime-free loam suits these heaths. They appreciate humus and full exposure. Short summer cuttings struck under a bell-glass.

CAMELLIA. Much hardier than is generally supposed, the many varieties of C. japonica are admirable shrubs for a lime-free soil, and they will prosper in places too shady for most shrubs. They like a good loam, enriched with leafy compost. No pruning required. A selection should include Adolph Adusson, Arijishii, Donckelarii in crimson-scarlet; the rose-pink Lady Clare, Preston Rose and Gloire de Nantes ; and the white nobilissima and White Swan. C. cuspidata is an elegant, small-leaved slender shrub of 6–8 ft. with sprays of white flowers suggesting orange blossom. A hardy and attractive addition to the family. Cuttings.

CARPENTERIA CALIFORNICA. A beautiful Californian evergreen with 2–3-in. creamy-white, scented, anemone-like flowers (July). Usually seen as a bush of 6 ft. or so, but grows taller in favourable localities. Should have a wall where winters are bleak. Average well-drained soil. Cuttings or seed. Ladham's Variety has larger, more fragrant flowers.

CARYOPTERIS MASTACANTHUS. The " blue spiræa " has been superseded by the hybrid C. clandonensis (see p. 119).

CEANOTHUS (EVERGREEN). Though not hardy, many of these, the loveliest of beautiful blue-flowered shrubs, will winter safely against a wall in all but the coldest localities. The bright blue C. dentatus and Russellianus, papillosus, Veitchianus and the early violet-blue rigidus (with its fine variety grandifolius) still hold their own, but are rivalled by such new hybrids as Delight, Autumnal Blue and the powder-blue Burkwoodii. The last, only 3–4 ft., is a late bloomer and perhaps the most beautiful of all. The others will make 6–10 ft. or more. A light, stony soil with full sun. Shorten back flowering ends as blooms go off. Cuttings.

CEANOTHUS (DECIDUOUS). The deciduous hybrids are generally hardier than the above. They are late bloomers and at their best against a west wall to which they may be trained, reducing all new wood except leaders in spring to near base. Flower panicles larger than those of evergreens, richest blues being Henri Defosse and Indigo ; medium to pale blues, Gloire de Versailles, Topaz and Arnoldii; pinks, Marie Simon, Richesse, roseus carmineus. Light, free soil. Cuttings. Sun.

CERATOSTIGMA WILLMOTTIANUM. The best of the plumbagos but not quite hardy. A charming shrub for the base of a sunny wall with a light soil. About 3 ft. as a bush, but trained against a wall it may make 10 ft. Flowers are a brilliant sky-blue and maintained from June to November. Rooted off-sets. Cut to base oldest branches, spring.

CERCIS SILIQUASTRUM. The Judas-tree is one of the most beautiful of the later spring. It grows to 30 ft. or more, but often seen flowering as quite a small shrub. Rose-pink pea-flowers closely cluster the naked twigs and branches, and the translucent green leaves colour well in autumn. Needs all possible sun and a good honest loam. No pruning.

CHERRY, see Prunus.

CHIMONANTHUS FRAGRANS. Familiar for centuries as "winter-sweet," this 6–10-ft. shrub yields, November to March, deliciously fragrant pale yellow and purple flowers on its naked branches. The variety grandiflorus is a better yellow but hardly so sweetly scented. Both are happier against a sunny wall. Layers or seed.

CHOISYA TERNATA. Known as Mexican orange, this is a hardy and useful evergreen with aromatic trefoil leaves and (March to June) corymbs of 1–1½-in. white, fragrant blossoms. There is often a second yield in autumn. Average height about 7 ft. with a wide spread. Should have a free soil and sun, but will do almost anywhere, even under trees. Cuttings, suckers or self-layered branches.

CISTUS. The rock roses comprise a number of beautiful evergreen shrubs well adapted for sunny mixed borders or dry slopes of poor soil. Though they last but a day or so, the flowers are borne in such profusion that their fleeting nature is of no moment. The two colours that prevail are white and mallow-rose, those of the former often having a bold flare of crimson at the base of the petals. Many rock roses are only half-hardy, the most reliable being noted below. The species are best raised from seed; hybrids and colour forms from summer cuttings. Pruning unnecessary.

WHITE-FLOWERED. One of the hardiest and most beautiful is C. cyprius, trustworthy almost anywhere. This fine hybrid rises to 6–10 ft. and its 3-in. white blossoms, with blood-red blotches, are yielded in prodigal luxuriance. C. laurifolius, with unspotted blooms in tall panicles and one of the few really hardy rock roses, is a bush of 6 ft. across, and another striking species is C. ladaniferus, the gum-cistus (see p. 94). This is on the tender side, but will stand average winters in our milder parts. Its 3-in. maroon-blotched white flowers are singularly lovely, and there are of both this and cyprius self-white varieties of the utmost loveliness. C. lusitanicus, a tolerably hardy and semi-prostrate bush of 3–4 ft., bears white flowers with carmine flares, and much like it, but taller, is C. glaucus (see p. 106) with similar flowers but narrower aromatic leaves. C. populifolius var. lasiocalyx is magnificent with its large milk-white blooms against a bold apple-green foliage. C. Aguilare, a new hybrid

75

from the last-mentioned and the pure white gum-cistus, is also a large-flowered white of great promise, and among the smaller-flowered self-whites worth noting are corbariensis and salvifolius (see Rock Plants).

COLOURED. C. Silver Pink is a hardy little hybrid with very large blooms in shrimp-pink, and Skanbergii (3–4 ft.) is distinct in bearing rose-pink blossoms. Other coloured sorts include the rosy-mauve crispus with its carmine-rose variety, Sunset, and the beautiful purpureus with large flat rosy-red blooms, each petal having a crimson blotch. This is one of the finest of all, but is not one of the hardiest. C. albidus, with white-felted leaves and silvery-mauve blossoms, is more trustworthy and attains 3 ft. or so. For smaller rock roses see "Halimium" under Rock Plants.

CLEMATIS. The loveliest of all climbing plants, clematises include a vast number of species and hybrids of inestimable garden value. They like a good loamy soil, preferably with lime, and while the lower parts should be in shade, the upper enjoy sun. May be grown on walls, garden arches or over old trees.

C. ARMANDII. A beautiful bold-leaved evergreen of robust growth. The 2-in. sweetly scented white flowers are produced in massive clusters in spring. Snowdrift is an outstanding form, and there are some charming rose-tinted varieties, notably Apple Blossom.

C. MACROPETALA (see p. 118). Dwarfer than most, this charming clematis is admirable for a low wall or terrace balustrade. In May and June it yields in abundance 3-in. downy blossoms usually in some shade of blue or violet with a paler centre. Markhami is a note-worthy clear pink. Will do on a shady wall.

C. MONTANA. A vigorous climber, producing a wealth of white, often rosy-tinted, blossoms in May. The rose-pink variety, rubens, even more beautiful. These are at their best rambling over an old tree or garden room. An easy plant under any conditions.

Others well worth noting are the rosy-white C. chrysocoma; Durandii, a semi-scandent hybrid, with large deep blue flowers; the white Spooneri and such varieties of C. viticella as the deep crimson Kermesina and alba luxurians, both mid-season to late.

LARGE-FLOWERED HYBRIDS. A selection of these should include the Lanuginosas, Beauty of Worcester, violet-blue; Lady Northcliff, rich lavender; Nelly Moser, rosy-white, carmine bars; William Kennett, lavender-blue. In the Jackman section, Jackmanii, deep violet-blue, purple or white; Mdme. E. Andre, bright velvety red; Perle d'Azur, light blue; Comtesse de Bouchard, satiny rose; Prince of Wales, burgundy. Among the Patens group are Edouard Defosse, deep mauve; Fair Rosamond, blush-white; Miss Bateman, white, chocolate centre; President, claret; and Lasurstern (see p. 96), bright blue-lavender. In pruning these hybrids the Jackmanii class and the stronger lanuginosas should be cut to within 18 in. of the ground in March. Patens vars. require only light pruning.

CLETHRA DELAVAYI. The handsomest of the sweet peppers, making an erect shrub of 8 ft., bearing, July to September, massive spikes of pure white bowl-shaped flowers with striking black anthers. Others worth noting are C. alnifolia paniculata and C. barbinervis with 6-in. spikes of fragrant white flowers in autumn and only some 4–5 ft. C. Fargesii is the tallest of all, 10–12 ft., a July-August bloomer, the long and elegant racemes being white and sweet-scented. A cool, lime-free soil for these valuable late bloomers. Sun or light shade.

CLIANTHUS PUNICEUS. Perhaps the most gorgeous of all climbing plants, the glory-pea is a wonderful spectacle when carrying its early summer crop of large lobster-claw flowers in a brilliant scarlet. Should have a warm wall, lightly shaded in south, and a free, gritty soil. Will reach 10 ft. or more. Handsome even as an evergreen, the large leaves being pinnate, or fern-like.

CORNUS KOUSA. The dogwoods include some admirable flowering trees of moderate stature, and the Japanese Kousa is one of the best, having 1–2-in. blush-white flowers from May to July. The leaves develop rich autumn tints. C. Nuttallii, an American, is superior even to the foregoing. The rosy-white flowers (bracts) are 3–4 in. across, spicily fragrant and borne in great abundance on established trees. In autumn the foliage assumes brilliant colours. As an early bloomer the old Cornelian cherry (C. Mas.) deserves notice, for its naked branches will not fail to be lit in February and March with a glittering array of little mustard-yellow blossoms. This and other cornels prosper in any good average soil. An occasional thinning of congested branches may be desirable.

COROKIA COTONEASTER. The select little New Zealand genus Corokia is represented here by its hardiest species, C. Cotoneaster. This is usually seen as a bush of 3–4 ft. with a tangle of wiry interlacing twigs, the leaves being small and few. In May it becomes ablaze with bright yellow star-shaped flowers which are followed by orange-red berries. A dry, poor soil, with sun, is all this interesting plant asks. No pruning.

CORYLOPSIS. A family related to the witch-hazels, and among its more attractive members C. pauciflora and spicata deserve special mention as under-middle-sized shrubs with a quiet beauty of their own and which are in flower in early spring when blossoms are few. Both are slenderly built, the latter not more than 3 ft., and the flowers that throng the leafless twigs are a clear yellow and cowslip-scented. A sunny spot with a light soil, and if the plants are on a bank, so that the flowers are seen from below, so much the better. No pruning.

COTONEASTER. This great family has little claim to make among flowering shrubs, most of its members being grown for their autumn–winter berry or leaf-colour. In these respects note should be taken of C. conspicua, Franchetii, the tree-like frigida Vicarii, Henryana, horizontalis, lactea, pannosa, salicifolia and Watereri. Indifferent as to soil or site, the cotoneasters have purposes to fulfil in every garden.

CRABS. See Malus.

CRATÆGUS. Like the cotoneasters, the hawthorns are mainly berrying shrubs, but the coloured forms of our own " may " (C. oxyacanthoides) are widely appreciated in gardens on account of their ease of culture under any conditions and wealth of cheerful blossom in spring. Paul's Scarlet is one of the best doubles, with plena rosea, double pink, close up. A good single scarlet is punicea, and rosea is a beautiful single rose-pink.

CYDONIA LAGENARIA. This name now covers the beautiful Japanese quince, long familiar as Pyrus japonica. There are no more valuable early bloomers than the varieties of this cousin of the apples, many of which, though they will do in the open, are suitable for quite low walls. A sunless aspect does not come amiss to them and they will tolerate most soils. The richly coloured Knaphill Scarlet and the salmon-crimson cardinalis comprise a brace of the best, but the semi-double warm flesh-pink Phylis Moore, the soft salmon-scarlet Rowallane Seedling and Moerloësii in apple-blossom pink should be noted.

CYTISUS ALBUS. The white Portugal broom is one of the loveliest of its family. It attains 6–7 ft. and its showers of whiplash branches wreathed with white flowers in May are beyond praise. A splendid shrub for poor hot soils, or as a background to heaths. Grouping extensively is not expensive, as it comes very easily from seed sown in the open.

C. BATTANDIERI. A striking new introduction with broad silvery trefoil leaves, which are evergreen, and (June) 4–5-in. racemes of yellow, pineapple-scented flowers. Quite hardy and will speedily attain 15 ft. or so. Seed. Prune lightly, merely to preserve shapeliness.

C. NIGRICANS. A shrub of 3–4 ft. which is especially useful since it flowers July to September. Has a bushy habit, and the erect racemes, 6–9 in., are bright yellow. Previous year's wood should be cut back in spring.

C. PURGANS. An old plant but still holding its own among the lesser brooms. It grows stiffly erect, the grey-green rush-like twigs bearing golden-yellow, fragrant flowers in abundance from April to June.

C. SCOPARIUS. The common broom needs no recommendation. In itself and its ivory-yellow variety, Moonlight, it is singularly beautiful, but the more typical yellows have been somewhat eclipsed by the varieties Andreanus, crimson and yellow; Burkwoodii, glowing wallflower-crimson; Daisy Hill Splendens, yellow and rose; Lord Lambourne, crimson and yellow; and many others. Then among hybrids are such outstanding brooms as the crimson-scarlet, gold and rose Geoffrey Skipwith, the lilac-rose Mrs. Norman Henry and the brilliant Johnson's Crimson, a newcomer, these last all having the slender grace and smaller flowers in lavish profusion of the white broom. C. præcox is also a hybrid of like character, but only about 4 ft. and bushier. It is very beautiful when laden with its creamy-yellow, richly scented blossoms. The Porlock broom also merits notice, for it is virtually a hardy "Genista fragrans" and flowers in spring, often continuing to autumn. Bright yellow, 5–10 ft.

No special culture needed for brooms in general. They thrive in any free soil, no matter how lean, with full sun. Varieties of scoparius and the hybrids should have flowering sprays cut back as soon as blooms go off.

DAPHNE MEZEREUM. This valuable early bloomer, its twigs crowded with crimson-purple very fragrant flowers from February to April, is a shrub for every garden, whether grown singly or in groups. The flowers are succeeded by scarlet berries, and there is an autumn-flowering variety, grandiflora, and a charming white (early spring) with yellow berries. Easily raised from seed. Average loam, not too stiff, sun or part shade. Height 4–5 ft., but flowering begins when only 6 in. No pruning.

Other attractive and reliable daphnes include D. acutiloba, 4–5 ft., white flowers (July) and large scarlet fruits; Burkwoodii, neatly rounded bush of about 3 ft. clustered in spring with rosy-flesh fragrant flowers; tangutica, a dense dark-leaved evergreen bearing (March-May) posies of rose-purple. See Rock Garden section.

DENDROMECON RIGIDUM. The beautiful tree poppy of California, though not hardy in inland places, may be planted with confidence in most maritime counties. It should be against a S. or W. wall in a meagre, light soil. The narrow leaves are grey-green and the fragrant, golden poppy flowers borne all summer at the tips of the branches. Will train up to 10–15 ft. Remove old and spent wood occasionally to base in spring. Cuttings.

DESFONTAINEA SPINOSA. One of the most gorgeous shrubs in our gardens, this grows to about 6 ft. with a wide spread. It has holly-like leaves and, in summer, is aflame with 2-in. waxen trumpets, brilliant scarlet-vermilion with a yellow lip. Not very hardy, but will stand average winters in our milder localities, or by seaside. A medium to light, lime-free soil, with humus; full sun or part shade. No pruning. Cuttings.

DEUTZIA. A graceful, free-flowering genus of hardy shrubs deserving more recognition than they now enjoy. The flowers are borne in elegant drooping panicles on slender leaning branches in spring and summer, and the plants, ranging from 3 ft. to 8 ft., do well in ordinary well-drained soil. A selection might consist of corymbosa, discolor major, gracilis, magnifica, scabra and Vilmorinæ, all whites; kalmiiflora, longifolia the rosy plum-purple Magician (see p. 118), scabra plena, Veitchii, blush to pink and rose-purple. Prune out flowering ends and old worn-out branches after blooming. Cuttings or rooted off-sets.

DIERVILLA (WEIGELA). A valuable group of hardy shrubs, under medium height with elegantly arched branches, laden (May-June) with showy tubular flowers. Rosea, Abel Carrière, Bouquet Rose, Eva Rathke, Fleur de Mai, Othello, styriaca, all good sorts, from pink to rich crimson-carmine; Candida is a fine white and Middendorfiana an early sulphur-yellow. Rich, moist soil. Remove all shoots after they have flowered. Cuttings.

ELEAGNUS MACROPHYLLA. The choicest of the oleasters making a large rounded bush of 8 ft. or so. The broad green leaves are silvered on the reverse, and the young shoots and little fuchsia-like flowers also silvery. These blossoms not particularly showy, but they are borne in November when others are few and have a sweet vanilla fragrance. Average soil; sun or part shade; no pruning needed.

EMBOTHRIUM COCCINEUM. The most brilliant of all flowering trees, the Chilean fire bush is an evergreen of 30 ft. or so. In May it is aflame with large clusters of honeysuckle-like flowers in a dazzling scarlet. Needs a non-limy, humous soil. Not suited to bleak localities. In many gardens the variety longifolium and semi-evergreen later introductions are more satisfactory and flower at an earlier age.

ENKIANTHUS. A small family of slender ericaceous shrubs of 4–8 ft. with an erect habit and clusters of drooping, bell-shaped flowers in spring. The foliage develops gorgeous autumn tints. The creamy-white campanulatus and cernuus, the ruby-red cernuus rubens, rosy-red Palibinii and pale primrose pallidiflorus are among the choicest. No lime; cool, free soil, with humus; seed, off-sets. Pruning unnecessary.

ERICA ARBOREA. This tall tree-like heath has a grey-green foliage and fragrant white flowers throng the long, tapering growths in spring. In all save the mildest districts its hardy and dwarfer form, alpina, should be grown instead.

E. AUSTRALIS. Another tree-heath of about 6 ft., bearing in May clusters of large bells in a vivid rose. One of the finest of the heaths, but not reliably hardy in inland gardens.

The white variety, Mr. Robert, is rather more trustworthy and is doubtless the most beautiful of all white heathers. These and the foregoing should have flowering ends cut back when blooming ceases.

E. CARNEA. This winter-flowering, mat-forming heath is an indispensable shrub. Perfectly hardy and easy, even on lime, it is first-rate whether grown singly or in drifts, and it asks no cultural attention. Its many colours range from the crimson Vivellii (see Rock Garden section) and Ruby Glow, through the rosy lilacs of King George, Queen Mary, J. Backhouse and atrorubra to the brilliant Springwood Pink. The finest white is Springwood, a most remarkable heath.

E. CILIARIS. The Dorset heath (see Rock Garden section) is at its best in the rose-crimson Maweana; globosa, rose pink; and the white Stoborough. These are erect but dwarf, or semi-trailing, with a glaucous moss-green foliage, and they flower from midsummer to autumn. A cool but free soil.

E. CINEREA. A selection of the popular bell-heather should not omit Apple Blossom, pale blush; atrorubens, ruby-red; C. D. Eason, fine ruby-crimson; the dwarf Mrs. Dill, carmine-rose; Rose Queen (see Rock Garden section). Most of these make bushy plants of a foot or so. They flower profusely throughout the later summer and are content with a drier soil than most.

E. HYBRIDA. Among the many hybrid heaths, making bushes of 12–18 in., are the winter-flowering darleyensis in rose-lilac; the bright rose-purple Dawn; H. Maxwell, rich pink; and Watsonii, large rose bells, all late summer. Another hybrid worth noting is Veitchii (arborea + lusitanica) with fragrant white bells in luxuriance in spring. Will grow to 6–7 ft.

E. LUSITANICA. A tree-heath with a bright green plumose foliage. An erect grower of 8 ft. or more, its fox-tail boughs are loaded with rosy-white flowers in winter and spring. Hardy in most places, provided soil is light. Well worth a trial even as an evergreen, its foliage being singularly attractive.

E. MEDITERRANEA. One of the hardiest of tree-heaths with a dark green foliage, erect growth and height of 6–8 ft. The honey-scented flowers are rose-lilac and carried in copious trusses (April–June). Best variety is superba, but the dwarf, Brightness, rosy-red, and the white, W. T. Rackcliff, should not be overlooked. Easy doers in a light to medium soil.

E. TERMINALIS. The Corsican heath, the hardiest of the taller species, will make 6 ft. Erect in growth, it has a beautiful plumose foliage in a soft green and is flushed from July onwards with its rosy bells. A good drought resister for thin soils. Makes a delightful hedge.

E. TETRALIX. Much like the common bell-heather in size and habit but earlier and does with a moister soil. Its foliage often glaucous, especially in the white-belled mollis. Pink Glow is another good variety, and Ruby's Variety, in a darker tint, a valuable late bloomer.

E. UMBELLATA. A trailing heath from Spain with a pleasing moss-green foliage and round carmine-rose blossoms in luxuriance during May. Not hardy in our coldest localities. Should be given a dry, stony soil.

E. VAGANS. The Cornish heath, one of the most ornamental of the family, is invaluable as a late bloomer. With a height of about 2 ft. or more it will spread to a width of some 6 ft., making a shapely mound. The typical rose-lilac superseded by the following fine varieties : St. Keverne, vivid rose-pink, long spikes; Mrs. Maxwell, deep cerise; and Lyonesse with white trusses. Tolerably hardy and easily grown in a medium loam.

All the above heaths (except carnea) should have a lime-free soil, preferably to the light side and freely drained. May be given some peat or vegetable compost when planted, but afterwards can be left alone. They enjoy an open situation and most of them are best grouped in generous drifts. Species from seed; hybrids and colour vars., short summer cuttings under bell-glass.

ESCALLONIA. A group of evergreen and deciduous shrubs, dwarf, medium and large. The evergreens best for seaside gardens, but several are hardy enough for most places, noteworthy among them being the crimson C. F. Ball; Slieve Donard and edinensis, pink; macrantha, rosy red; Iveyana, the best white. The finest non-evergreen is langleyensis, with whiplash branches wreathed with carmine-rose flowers. Most of these are summer bloomers and very adaptable as to soil and situation. Cuttings.

EUCRYPHIA CORDIFOLIA and **E. GLUTINOSA.** See pp. 103 and 93.

E. NYMANSAY. A beautiful hybrid between the above species and well worthy of them. More vigorous than its parents and evergreen, it soon runs up in column shape to 15–20 ft. The flowers, bowl-shaped, 2 in. across, are pure white with a freckling of dark anthers, and a succession is maintained from July to autumn. A good loamy soil, non-limy and enriched with humus for this choice tree (see p. 110).

EUONYMUS. Although the spindlewoods make no pretence to be flowering trees and shrubs they contribute so bountiful a share of autumn colour with their brilliant fruits and leaf tints that we cannot pass them by. The best of them are deciduous and range from 6 ft. to 10 ft. or more, the large swinging fruits being in some shade of coral, scarlet and blood-red, and there are one or two whites. Our choice would include E. alatus, mainly for leaf colour; europæus, in several varieties; latifolius; planipes; yedoënsis. Will thrive in any ordinary loam, including lime. Cuttings; seed; no pruning.

EUPATORIUM MICRANTHUM. A soft-wooded Mexican, quite reasonably hardy in a light soil, if treated like a herbaceous plant by cutting back to base in spring. A round bush of some 4–5 ft. with glossy leaves and copious masses of fragrant foamy inflorescences in early autumn. A favourite butterfly shrub. Cuttings.

EXOCHORDA. A genus of charming spring-flowering shrubs, up to 12 ft., with the grace and foliage of a willow and large panicles of snow-white flowers. The latter often accompany the pretty amber and dove-coloured young foliage and they are produced in abundance year after year. E. Giraldii (see p. 123), Wilsonii, macrantha and racemosa make a choice quartette. Full sun and a moist loam. Seed.

FABIANA IMBRICATA. An interesting and beautiful member of the potato tribe with a heathy foliage and tubular white flowers in late spring. Will grow to 6–8 ft. Will not stand severe frost, but the newer F. violacea, with violet trumpets, is more resisting and a delightful plant. Light soil, with sun. Cuttings.

FORSYTHIA. Spring-flowering shrubs which have won a wide popularity on account of their ease of culture under normal conditions and their wealth of daffodil-yellow flowers on the leafless twigs. The flowering season opens in February with F. ovata, which is followed by suspensa and its variety atrocaulis, the deep golden-yellow intermedia spectabilis and suspensa Sieboldii. Flowering twigs should be cut back when blooming ceases.

FREMONTIA CALIFORNICA. A magnificent Californian that will ascend to a dozen feet against a warm wall. Not a shrub for bleak localities. Often does well near the sea. The thick leaves, dull green, hairy and lobed, are semi-evergreen and the large mallow-like flowers, a deep, highly burnished golden-yellow with orange stamens, are abundantly yielded, May to September. A light gravelly, or sandy, soil recommended. No pruning. Not difficult to raise from seed.

FUCHSIA. Most of the F. magellanica group are hardy, one of the tallest and best being Riccartonii. Other good sorts are corallina, globosa, gracilis, Thomsonii and the almost white alba, one of the best. Very accommodating, will do in any free soil, even in shade. Cut to base in spring if frost injured.

GARRYA ELLIPTICA. A striking, highly ornamental and hardy Californian evergreen, making a large bush, even in the poor soil it seems to favour. Its primary features are the clusters of emerald-grey and yellow drooping catkins it bears in mid-winter, those on male trees often being 10–15 in. long. A good seaside evergreen.

GENISTA ÆTNENSIS. The tallest of the brooms, rising slenderly to 15–18 ft., its fine rush-like twigs falling in a shower of emerald-green. This veil of twigs is dappled in August with little yellow, very fragrant flowers. A most beautiful and graceful broom and hardy. Any average to light soil, with sun. Seed.

G. CINEREA. One of the choicest of all, and especially valuable as a July-August bloomer. Makes about 8 ft. ; its silvery green, silky twigs, elegantly arched, carry a profusion of golden-yellow blossoms, and it is a good doer in a light warm soil with full sun. Cuttings.

G. VIRGATA. This striking Madeiran is akin to cinerea but more erect, more bushy and more leafy. Foliage is silvered with silk, and the yellow flowers (June–July) are borne in small racemes in abounding luxuriance. Will grow to 10 ft., but is often no more than 6 ft. in a poor, lean soil, which is recommended. Seed.

GREVILLEA. None of the grevilleas are really hardy, but G. rosmarinifolia and G. sulphurea will stand average winters in many localities, especially if grown in a free soil on a breezy, elevated site. The evergreen leaves are narrow, almost linear, and the curious flowers, without any petals, crimson in the one and ivory-yellow in the other, are borne from early spring onwards. Usually seen as shrubs of 2–3 ft., but sulphurea is taller and more erect. Should be grouped and associated with such as heaths. Cuttings strike easily.

HALESIA CAROLINA. The N. American snowdrop-tree, which does not exceed 8–12 ft., is a lovely object in May and June when its slender branches are hung with white bells. One of the most elegant of all small trees and a worthy successor to the cherries. A rarer, much larger species, with 1-in. bells of purest white, is H. monticola, also of U.S.A.

HAMAMELIS MOLLIS. The best of the witch-hazels and a glorious object when its naked boughs are tasselled with rich gold, spicy blossoms, these prevailing from December to March. Also winter-flowering are H. japonica, jap. arborea and vernalis. These and mollis make large open-habited shrubs or small trees. They are quite hardy and give no trouble under average conditions.

HIBISCUS SYRIACA. The tree-hollyhock merits more attention than it receives, for its mallow flowers appear from August onwards, and there are many colours among them, ranging from white to blush, rose-pink, red, crimson, lilac, purple and blue, singles and doubles. H. syriaca is quite hardy and makes a bushy shrub up to 7–10 ft. high. It should have a well-drained soil and the sunniest position. Can be increased by cuttings or layers. No pruning.

HOHERIA LYALLII GLABRATA. See p. 117.

HYDRANGEA OPULOIDES. This worthy old garden plant is widely appreciated, but the varieties of the Mariesii group, with flat corymbs surrounded by large bracts, white, pink or blue, deserve to be better known. H. paniculata (see p. 106), with white trusses ageing to pink, is a charming woodland shrub, and among many others the handsome H. quercifolia arrests attention (see p. 115). Hydrangeas come very readily from cuttings and prosper in ordinary garden soil in sun or shade.

HYPERICUM PATULUM. This, in its varieties Henryi and Forrestii, is the best of the taller hypericums. They are indispensable shrubs where late colour is desired, for they yield their wide golden-yellow salvers in profusion from August to the first frosts. H. Rodgersii is even larger in flower and richer in colour, but rather tender. The familiar H. calycinum is invaluable as a woodland carpeter and the 1-ft. Moserianum an excellent shrub for the front of the border. Free soil, sun. Cuttings.

INDIGOFERA. A genus of pea-flowered shrubs, some of which are hardy and very attractive in bloom. One of the most desirable and trustworthy is I. Gerardiana, 5–6 ft., bearing panicles of bright rosy blossoms, July to September. May be cut back to base in spring. Another reliable and pretty species with a longer flowering season is the rose-lilac I. Potaninii.

JASMINUM NUDIFLORUM. The familiar winter jasmine has long held the affection of all gardeners by its thorough reliability in any soil, in sun or shade. One of the most carefree of shrubs. J. officinale, with sweetly scented white flowers, an elegant manner and foliage, is useful for clambering over an old tree or garden arch.

KALMIA LATIFOLIA. This American is one of the most beautiful of all flowering shrubs. Makes 5–6 ft., has an attractive foliage, and the flowers (June), borne in ample clusters, are angular-saucer-shaped, waxen and a delicious pink. Non-limy, humous soil. No pruning.

KALMIOPSIS LEACHIANA. Still a rare plant but coming to the front rapidly now that its hardiness and high garden value are being realised. A N.W. American evergreen of 1 ft., it enjoys a humous soil, cool and light, but not too dry. The little kalmia-like blossoms in a keen wild-rose pink are borne from spring onwards. A shrublet for associating with choice ericaceæ. Cuttings.

LABURNUM. Long familiar but still holding its own as one of the loveliest of spring bloomers. In addition to the common kind, L. alpinum is noteworthy as a late flowerer with 9–12 in. racemes, and Vossii is a first-rate hybrid with still longer ropes of blossom and a bold foliage.

LEIOPHYLLUM BUXIFOLIUM. The N. American sand-myrtle is the choicest of the ledum fraternity. A bonny little compact evergreen with small deep green leaves. In spring it is dappled with coral buds which break into a foam of rosy crystal blossoms. Admirable for an ericaceous border or any cool soil. Hardy and trouble-free (see p. 120).

LEPTOSPERMUM. The south-sea myrtles are not generally hardy but cannot be passed over, for they are so eminently graceful in their wispy lightness, so lavish in their blossoming from May to July. The L. scoparium group the most attractive, including the typical white, the pink Chapmanii and ruby-crimson Nichollsii, with its excellent variety, gloriosa. Light, poor soil, full sun. Cuttings.

LONICERA. The honeysuckles enjoy a universal appreciation. With a cool soil for the roots and their heads in the sun they will do under most conditions. The climbers the most important. Bush varieties chiefly notable for the winter blooming: Standishii and fragrantissima, both very sweet, the fragrant rose-lilac syringantha (June) and pyrenaica, a charming little bush of 3–4 ft. with ivory bells, deliciously scented. Among the finest climbers are L. japonica Halliana, primrose from May onwards; Early and Late Dutch, red to yellow trumpets; the orange-scarlet sempervirens; Tellmanniana and tragophylla, the last two bearing very large flowers, bronzy yellow.

MAGNOLIA. This magnificent family includes shrubs for small gardens and trees for larger spaces. In the former the 4–6-ft. M. stellata (see p. 122) is lovely in spring, its white, or rosy, ribboned blossoms, sweet-scented, being yielded in prodigal luxuriance. M. parviflora (see p. 111) is no less worthy later on, while the big-flowered liliflora, white and wine red, and the deep purple, nigra, are also comparatively slow growing and under middle size. Among the taller growers is the superb Campbellii (see p. 97) ; the waxen-white denudata ; Kobus, with widely strap-shaped white petals ; the purple and white Lennei (see p. 124) ; salicifolia, akin to Kobus and equally beautiful; the handsome purple Soulangeana with a lovely white; Watsonii with large, flat, crimson-centred white blooms ; and Wilsonii, cup-shaped, white with crimson anthers. These are all richly fragrant. They will prosper in any good loam and need no attention, but a yearly top-dressing with compost is helpful when young.

MAHONIA. The mahonias, once among berberis, are back again in a genus of their own, and the most generally useful is the old M. aquifolium, with its clusters of lemon-yellow (March to May) and blue-purple fruits. A shrub of many forms, it is most useful as an undergrowth for thin woodland or carpeting the ground under trees. M. Bealei is a fine species with massive leaves and bold cockades of lemon-yellow fragrant flowers in spring, and M. japonica is close up in merit with rather less upright racemes in the same colour. M. nepalensis is another striking shrub in the same style, but not so hardy as Bealei, the most reliable of its class. All can be cut down to near ground (spring) when leggy.

MALUS. The flowering crabs comprise some trees and shrubs of the highest merit. Most of them follow the cherries from late April to June, and they are easily grown in any average soil. A short list should include M. Eleyi, wine-red with crimson young leaves; floribunda, pink flowers on drooping branches, one of the best; purpurea, deep crimson; Schiedeckeri, semi-double rose and white. No pruning necessary.

MUTISIA. Climbing Chilean shrubs and interesting as being among the very few climbing composites. The finest is M. decurrens which has the habit of a perennial pea, producing in full summer large, broadly rayed blossoms in a flaming vermilion-scarlet. Should have its roots on the shady side of a bush with some support for its tendrils. Hardier and more generally adaptable are the rose to pale blush M. retusa and oligodon. Seed; rooted offsets.

NANDINA DOMESTICA. A bamboo-like shrub of 5–6 ft. With long, narrowly fingered leaves which are highly coloured when young and again in autumn. About mid-summer pyramidal panicles of white flowers appear at the extremities and these are followed by scarlet fruits. Medium peaty soil; sheltered situation; light shade.

NEILLIA LONGIRACEMOSA. See p. 116.

OLEARIA. O. Gunniana, with white daisy-flowers, is the most ornamental of the hardier of these grey-leaved Antipodeans, and its coloured forms are very charming but more tender. The only reasonably hardy species is Haastii, which has been more freely planted than it merits. O. macrodonta (white) and the beautiful semi-dentata (mauve) may be added to Gunniana as possibles for seaside gardens or mild localities. Cuttings and seed.

OSMANTHUS DELAVAYI. A beautiful shrub of 4–6 ft. with small dark-green leaves and daphne-like white flowers, richly scented, in spring. A singularly choice shrub and the best of the family. Not difficult in a free soil and sunny position. Flowers frost-tender. Cuttings.

OSMAREA BURKWOODII. The result of a cross between the above and Phillyrea decora. Resembles the osmanthus in its deep green, rather larger, leaves and clusters of white trumpet-flowers in spring, but grows more erect. An admirable shrub for an ornamental hedge. One of the best of evergreens for a dry, hot soil and quite hardy. Cuttings.

OXYDENDRUM ARBOREUM. One of the "andromedas." This is a choice N. American deciduous shrub of 10–15 ft. or more, but it will begin flowering when less than half grown. The handsome glossy leaves are exceedingly brilliant in autumn and the 6-in. panicles of white bell-like flowers are yielded from August onwards. A non-limy soil, cool and moist, with humus. A shrub to associate with rhododendrons, pieris and the like in thin woodland.

PERNETTYA MUCRONATA. Pleasing evergreen shrubs averaging 2–3 ft. that may be allowed to form a thicket under conditions suited to rhododendrons and heaths. The small leaves are deep green and glossy and white urn-shaped flowers are followed by large and brilliant fruits, yielded in dense clusters and ripening in autumn to prevail far into winter. These berries are singularly decorative, being pure white, blush, pink, lilac, crimson or purple. Bell's Seedling perhaps the best of the red-berried, and Davis' Hybrids give the finest range of colour varieties. Light, non-limy soil. Offsets. Do not plant where the shrub's inclination for suckering may lead to trouble.

PEROWSKIA ATRIPLICIFOLIA. This soft-wooded shrub is most useful as a late bloomer, especially on chalky soils which it seems to prefer. Both the 3-ft. wands that rise annually from the base after cutting back in spring (this is not necessary in genial climates) and the leaves are grey-white and form a telling setting for the spikes of intense violet blossoms. Light, stony soil; cuttings.

PHILADELPHUS. The mock oranges are among the most useful and ornamental of early summer shrubs. They will thrive anywhere, are perfectly hardy and the family embraces sizes to suit all gardens, their heights ranging from 2 ft. to 12 ft. Among the talls the old P. coronarius, heavily fragrant, the scentless grandiflorus, the new burfordiensis (see p. 104), Favourite, Virginal (double) and Norma are suggested, all white or cream. Medium sizes should include Fantaisie (see p. 100) ; Voie Lactée, white single; Burkwoodii, white flushed rose (see p. 112) ; Belle Etoile, white, purple centre. Many dwarfs are listed among the Lemoine Hybrids, and P. microphyllus, very sweet, will not exceed 2 ft. in a poor soil. Old wood and flowering ends pruned out when blooming ceases. Cuttings; rooted suckers.

PIERIS JAPONICA. The most generally grown of a beautiful family, this 5-6-ft. bush yields (March and April) pendulous racemes of fragrant white blossoms (see p. 121). Much like it, but leaves of a paler green and erect racemes, is P. taiwanensis, and formosa is a tall and handsome species (see p. 114) flowering rather later. P. Forrestii, allied to formosa, also a charming shrub. All have white flowers, and the brilliant colour of their young leafy shoots is a notable feature. Non-limy light soil with humus; part shade. Seed or layers.

POLYGONUM BALDSCHUANICUM. The Russian vine is now familiar as a tall and rampant climber with cascades of rosy-white in summer and autumn. A grand plant for enveloping an old tree or covering an unsightly building in quick time. A good loam, sunny position. Cuttings of soft wood in summer or woody portions in autumn-winter.

P. VACCINIFOLIUM. A creeping shrub that is extremely useful for carpeting woodland or draping banks in sun or shade. Rarely exceeds 6 in., and its pretty spikes of rose-pink in autumn are followed by a brilliant leaf-colour. Will do anywhere (said to resent lime), but thrives best in cool soil. Self-rooted layers easily procured for increase.

POTENTILLA. In addition to those given under Rock Plants, the following taller kinds should be noted : P. Friedrichsenii, bright yellow; Vilminoriana, silvery foliage, ivory primrose, throughout the season. Will prosper under any conditions.

PRUNUS (ALMONDS). The common almond (see p. 101), beautiful as it is, has been eclipsed by the magnificent hybrid, P. communis Pollardii (see p. 113), the flowers of which are 2 in. wide, a richer pink and more sweetly scented. Makes a small tree, hardy and easy in a medium loam. The double peaches, Cambridge Scarlet, Russell's Red and Clara Meyer, also among the best of ornamental stone-fruits.

PRUNUS (CHERRIES). The loveliest of spring-flowering trees, hardy and free under average conditions. A selection of ornamental cherries should include such whites as P. yedoënsis (see p. 107), incisa and Jo-nioi (both comparatively small in stature), Shirotae, semi-double, Tai-Haku and the double white gean. In pinks, Sieboldii, Kwanzan, J. H. Veitch, Hokusai and serrulata rosea are all good. Others to be earmarked by those who want the best are the pink P. subhirtella, its columnar form ascendans, the winter-flowering autumnalis and P. s. pendula and rosea, all supremely lovely. Most cherries should be grown as lawn specimens, but they are well adapted for mixed shrub borders, avenues and margins of woodland.

RHODODENDRON. The most beautiful of all flowering shrubs, this great family possesses garden qualifications of the highest, most of its members being hardy and care-free in any light to medium non-limy soil, enriched with leafy compost or peat. In sizes ranging from 2 ft. to 20 ft., and providing flowers in a wide variety of colours over a long period, they should appeal strongly to all having the right conditions. Most of the larger kinds appreciate light shade, but the smaller they are the more sun can they take is a general rule. From the hosts of species and varieties we can only offer one or two abbreviated personal selections from the well-tried, referring the reader to a good nursery list and the Rhododendron Association for further suggestions.

LARGE TO MEDIUM. R. campylocarpum, yellow; cinnabarinum, cinnabar-red, apricot, ruby-red; discolor, white or pink, late; Fargesii, rose-pink; Fortunei, pale rose; lutescens, yellow; orbiculare, vivid rose-pink; Thomsonii, deep blood-red.

MEDIUM TO SMALL. R. Augustinii, blue-lavender to harebell-blue; callimorphum, clear rose; glaucum, apple-blossom pink; Griersonianum, geranium-scarlet; mucronatum (see Azalea ledifolia, pp. 73 and 114); neriiflorum, blood-red; oreotrephes, silvery mauve to pale rose; racemosum, white to pink (see p. 110); Williamsianum, bright rose; yunnanense, white to rose-lilac (see p. 108).

HYBRIDS. Cornubia, bright blood-red; Earl of Athlone, blood-red; fastuosum fl. pl., violet; Luscombei, rich rose-pink; Loder's White (see p. 95); Mrs. E. C. Stirling, blush-white; præcox, rose-purple; Shilsonii, crimson-scarlet; Unique, rose-flushed apricot.

For dwarfs see Rock Garden section.

RIBES SANGUINEUM. The old flowering currant is one of the worthiest of spring shrubs and a healthy, contented plant anywhere. Atrorubens, Edward VII and splendens, best varieties. R. speciosum, also of California, is another member of the family of much garden value. It makes a large shrub, its branches being densely hung (April–May) with long, fuchsia-like, ruby-crimson flowers. Cuttings.

ROMNEYA COULTERI. See p. 105.

ROSA. Among roses of special merit, other than the H.T.'s, Ramblers, Bush Polyanthas, Hybrid Musks and others, descriptions of which are provided by the lists of specialists and N.R.S., the following are recommended :

R. ALBA. The old glaucous-leaved " White Rose of York." Easy-going, very fragrant and charming in all varieties, including the double blush-pink Celestial (see p. 122), the pale rosy-white, semi-double Maiden's Blush and the semi-double pure white. This is a bush rose for every garden; 5–8 ft. Remove spent wood occasionally.

R. CHINENSIS. Well known as the Chinese, or monthly, rose, this is a universal favourite, its single, double or semi-double blossoms being borne the season through, their colours ranging from white to pink and crimson-carmine. Best varieties are Comtesse du Cayla,

Fabvier, Fellemberg, Hermosa, Old Blush (see p. 98), Old Crimson. All bush roses of under medium height. Good for a light soil. Only gentle pruning needed.

R. HUGONIS. A lovely small-leaved rose of moderate size wreathed with clear yellow flowers May–June. The hybrid, cantabrigensis, is rather taller, paler yellow, equally prolific and more satisfactory in some soils. Should not require the knife.

R. MOYESII. The finest of all rose species, a tall and vigorous grower, yielding crimson-scarlet blossoms, rich and velvety, June–July. These followed by large brilliantly coloured heps. R. Fargesii, much like it, but with pink flowers, and such hybrids as Hillieri, high-downensis and the varieties Geranium and Maroon, all bear the hall-mark of Moyesii quality. No pruning.

R. RUBIGINOSA. Our well-loved sweet-briar has for most garden purposes been superseded by the Penzance Briars. This large group of hybrids, many having aromatic foliage, offers bush varieties, single and semi-double, in a great variety of delightful colours. Indifferent as to soil and require no attention. Old wood may be cut to base every year or so.

R. RUGOSA. A most useful and attractive section that will do well as bushes in the leanest of soil, yielding their fine flowers freely and succeeding them with large, highly coloured fruits. The handsome foliage brightly tinted in autumn. A short list should include Agnes, double, amber-yellow; Blanc Double de Coubert, double white; F. J. Grootendorst, deep pink, double, perpetual; Frau Dagmar Hartopp, single pink; Mrs. A. Waterer, semi-double, deep crimson; Parfum de l'Hay, double, mulberry-red. Cut out old and worthless wood in spring.

R. SPINOSISSIMA (SCOTCH ROSES). The burnets comprise some charming little thicket roses in white, yellow, rose and bicolors, most of them sweet-scented and invaluable for hot dry slopes and gravelly soils. The Scotch Roses, derived from them, are universal favourites, especially the old double yellow, but there are some good pinks and dwarfs of only 18 in. or so, notably the maroon-crimson, William III. All these are as accommodating as the true burnets and seldom need pruning.

In addition to the above the following are all distinct and of high garden merit: R. Andersonii, 4-in. rose-pink; Banksiæ, white and double-yellow (see p. 109), vigorous climbers for warm wall, very fragrant, thin only when essential; Davidii, pink, fine orange-red fruits; Dupontii, 3-in. pale pink, fragrant, thornless; macrantha, large shrub or pillar, 4-in. pink to white, scented; Mermaid, the well-known climber (or bush) with immense yellow blooms and fine foliage; Willmottiæ, graceful shrub, glaucous young wood, rose-lilac blossoms; xanthina, grey-green foliage, butter-yellow flowers.

RUBUS DELICIOSUS. A singularly beautiful Rocky Mt. raspberry with 5–8-ft. canes wreathed with 2-in. flowers like white wild roses, late May. Moist soil, part shade. Cut flowering canes to base soon as blooming ceases. Rooted off-sets.

SALVIA. The shrubby sages are not generally hardy, but they are such useful all-summer bloomers and so brightly coloured that no one who has the base of a S. or W. wall to offer them should pass them by. S. Grahami, red-crimson, is one of the best-known and much hardier than the very similar Greggii. It averages 3 ft. but taller when trained against a wall.

S. neurepia, the most pleasing for its broad-lipped blossoms are a pure scarlet. Will stand an average winter, with above protection. Cuttings; a reserve should be wintered in a cold frame.

SENECIO. A group of beautiful grey-leaved, golden daisy-flowered shrubs especially good for seaside gardens. Will do in a poor, stony soil. Prune hard when leggy, preferably after flowering. Noteworthy kinds among the hardiest are S. compacta, Greyi and Monroi, all 2-4 ft., widespread. Full sun. Cuttings.

SOLANUM CRISPUM. The best of the potato-flowered trees, this lovely Chilean makes a shapely bush of 10 ft. or more, and its variety autumnalis (Glasnevin) will yield clusters of blue-purple, orange-eyed blossoms from May to November. A mild climate or wall shrub. When trained should be pruned fairly hard in spring. Free soil; sun. Cuttings.

SPARTIUM JUNCEUM. This splendid old broom is one of the best of shrubs, easily raised from seed, ready to flourish in any light soil, any aspect, and to produce its fragrant clusters of " golden sweet peas " from June to September. Grows from 5 ft. to 10 ft. Flowering twigs may be shortened in spring, or the plant clipped over at that season so as to present a formal shrub. Should be generously grouped or given a place at back of shrub border.

SPIRÆA. The shrubby species include varieties of from 3 ft. to 15 ft., with flowering seasons that prevail from March to November. They like a non-limy soil, not too dry, and require no attention beyond the occasional removal of the older wood and flowering ends after blooming. Most of them provide rooted suckers in plenty. The following is a short list:

S. ARBOREA. Makes an enormous bush, very elegant with its fern-like leaves and 12-in. panicles of white foam in autumn. Lindleyana is closely akin.

S. ARGUTA. A gracefully arched slender shrub of 3-5 ft., sheeted with white flowers in April-May. S. canescens is much like it but taller and later. A valuable couple for limited spaces.

S. BRACTEATA. The handsomest of the June bloomers, its arched wands heavily padded with white clusters amid leaden-green leaves. Grows to about 6 ft. in a moist soil (see p. 102). Much like it is the newer trichocarpa, a taller shrub.

S. JAPONICA BUMALDA. This old hybrid is always welcome in the later summer with its broad corymbs of ruby-crimson. Anthony Waterer, one of the best forms; Walluff, a deeper colour and not so inclined to bleach. Should be grouped, preferably in light shade. Hard pruning in spring.

STACHYURUS PRÆCOX. This choice shrub makes an erect growth averaging about 6 ft. It is hardy and deciduous, the bark is a deep wine-red and this proves a telling setting for the pendulous racemes of lemon-yellow flowers that occur in early spring. These flowers are not large, but with their red calyces and the red stems they are singularly attractive. Any decent loam will serve and a sunny position is desirable. S. sinensis is an allied species, not quite up to præcox in merit. No pruning. Old branches may be removed occasionally.

MY GARDEN'S CHOICE

STRANVÆSIA DAVIDIANA. An attractive genus of evergreens of which one of the hardiest and most generally useful is S. Davidiana (see p. 120), with its near ally, salicifolia, and undulata close up in merit. The long narrow leaves are beautifully tinted in spring and autumn, the bold corymbs of flowers in June are white and followed by scarlet berries. Very willing and adaptable in a free soil, or may be used to cover sunless walls. Cuttings.

STUARTIA. A long-neglected but singularly beautiful family of N. American and Asiatic shrubs allied to camellia. Hardy and not difficult in a peaty or vegetable soil, cool and moist but well-drained, with occasional mulches of leafy compost. Roots should be shaded from hot sun. Cuttings may be struck in very sandy soil under a hand-light, late summer. A selection of the less rare and most reliable should include, S. pentagyna (8–10 ft.) creamy-white flowers, 3–4 in. across, late summer; S. p. grandiflora, with purple instead of yellow stamens to the wide white blossoms; S. pseudo-camellia (8–12 ft.) bowl-shaped milk-white flowers, yellow stamens, July; S. sinensis, taller than foregoing, smaller fragrant, cup-shaped blossoms in June. All the above are noted for their rich autumn tints.

STYRAX JAPONICUS. See p. 99.

SYRINGA. The lilacs have won the wide esteem they enjoy not only by reason of their old-world charm, beautiful colours and sweet fragrance, but through their willing good-nature, few shrubs being more indifferent to soil. To grow the garden varieties well they certainly need a rich soil, with annual mulching, but the species will thrive in any loam that is not too light. No systematic pruning required, but it is wise to remove the spent flower trusses.

Single or double varieties of the common lilac are numerous, and of them the nursery lists give faithful description. A good collection should not omit (singles) alba grandiflora, white; Charles X, deep purple; Mme. Francisque Morel, rosy lilac; Mont Blanc, large white; Souvenir de L. Spath, deep crimson; Vulcan, rich red-purple; (doubles) Charles Joly, dark red; Francisque Morel, bright rosy-violet; Leon Simon, blue; Mme. E. Harding, bright red-carmine; Mme. Lemoine, very large white; President Grevy, rosy-mauve. But some of the others must be noted here, among them being the Rouen lilac in several striking colours. The Persian lilac is a delightful shrub of only 4–5 ft., with lilac or white flowers; Syringa reflexa is distinct and handsome, with large leaves and trusses of pink, and tomentella, a robust shrub of 8–10 ft., is lovely when bearing its wide, branching panicles of very fragrant flesh-pink blossoms.

TAMARIX. A group of Old World deciduous shrubs notable for the elegance of their slender wispy growths, the fresh green of their minute leaves and crowded racemes of blossom in some shade of pink. Though especially partial to the seaside they may be grown in any decent loam that is well drained and make charming ornamental hedges. Propagation by cuttings, any "stick" thrust into the ground in autumn taking root. For general purposes T. gallica is recommended, but choicer kinds include T. hispida, glaucous foliage, pink blossom in autumn, 4 ft.; T. juniperina, spring flowering, very graceful, tall grower; T. pentandra, perhaps the hardiest, rosy plumes in August, 12 ft.; T. tetandra, racemes of bright pink in May. 10 ft.

TECOMA (BIGNONIA) (CAMPSIS). Climbing shrubs of high decorative merit. They need a lofty wall, since they will attain 20–30 ft., all possible sun and a hearty loam. T.

radicans, the most reliable, very handsome with its large fern-like leaves and 3-in. trumpets, scarlet and orange, in the later summer. Though a self-clinger it is better for some support. Rather less hardy is T. grandiflora, also with a bold pinnate leafage and orange-red trumpet flowers, 3 in. long, from August onwards. Like radicans, should be given wiring or trellis. When wall space is covered prune annually (spring) by cutting back side-shoots to couple of eyes of main stems. Layers.

TEUCRIUM FRUTICANS. The shrubby germander is a pretty evergreen shrub for a low wall or rambling over an old stump. Leaves are aromatic and bright green, but undersides, flower stalks and younger wood are white. The five-lobed, long-lipped flowers, borne all summer and autumn, bright lavender-blue. A violet-flowered form has been introduced, but it is tender. Sun or light shade; well-drained, light soil; cuttings strike easily.

TRICUSPIDARIA LANCEOLATA. One of the finest of the many Chilean introductions, making a small tree in mild districts. The leaves are evergreen, and from midsummer onwards the branches are thronged with pendulous urn-shaped blossoms in a full bright crimson. Not quite hardy everywhere. Does well on a N. side with a lime-free soil enriched with vegetable compost at planting time. Perhaps the most striking tree of its season. Comes readily from cuttings. No pruning.

ULEX EUROPÆUS FL. PL. The double gorse is a magnificent shrub when laden with its heavy trusses of fragrant yellow flowers. These flowers last longer than in the common gorse and the shrub is more compact and not so tall. An admirable thing for hot, arid slopes in full sun. Makes an appropriate companion for heaths. Easily raised from cuttings.

VACCINIUM. The whortleberries excel more highly in autumn leaf colour and berry than in blossom, but a few of them are generally ornamental. A selection should include V. corymbosum (4 ft.), with blush-white bells; glauco-album (4–6 ft.), evergreen leaves grey-green and blue-white underparts, racemes of rose-white flowers with frosty-emerald bracts followed by blue-powdered berries, not fully hardy; Mortinia, very charming evergreen, having leaves tinted with bronze and rose and pink bells, 2–4 ft.; ovatum, evergreen of 6–8 ft., glossy leaves, clusters of soft pink, Sept.–Oct.; padifolium, rather tender evergreen of 5–6 ft., wide bells, primrose with purple stains; pennsylvanicum (2 ft.), a pretty shrub with pink flowers and singularly vivid autumn leaf tints; virgatum (often listed as corymbosum), growing to some 4–5 ft., has pale rose blossoms, berries with a blue bloom and exceptionally fine autumn colour. All these like a moist, cool, lime-free soil not lacking humus and a place in the sun. No pruning necessary.

VERONICA. Few of the shrubby speedwells are hardy, but many do well in seaside gardens. They are not fastidious as to soil and most of them make shapely, compact bushes up to 5–6 ft. A selection of the more trustworthy should include Balfouriana, purple; Bowles' Hybrid, mauve; elliptica Autumn Glory, dwarf, violet; Gibbsii, dwarf, white; Mathewsii, violet and white; Traversii, mauve or white. In the large-flowered speciosa class, for genial climates only, there are some exceedingly ornamental varieties, notably Alicia Amherst, royal purple; La Suisante, bright crimson; Simon Deleaux, rich wine-crimson. All veronicas easily raised from cuttings.

VIBURNUM (EVERGREEN). The evergreen guelder-roses are comparatively few in flowering plants of merit. V. Burkwoodii, 6 ft., bearing (April–May) globular heads of blush-white blossoms, is one of the best; Davidii (see p. 102) is a bold-leaved, lowly, dome-shaped shrub with rosy-white clusters followed by blue berries; Henryi, loose panicles of white, red fruits, handsome foliage; rhytidophyllum, a noble large-leaved evergreen, striking heads of rosy flowers, red fruits, 12–15 ft.; V. Tinus (laurustinus), well worth a place in one or other of its best forms for winter flowering.

VIBURNUM (DECIDUOUS). Many beautiful viburnums in this section, including V. bitchiuense, flesh-pink, fragrant, late summer; Carlesii, 3–4 ft., one of the choicest of all flowering shrubs, with heads of rosy-white, deliciously scented flowers, spring; fragrans, perhaps the finest of winter-flowering shrubs, trusses of pale pink or white, 5–6 ft.; grandi-florum, larger in flower than fragrans, vivid rose, flowers frost-tender; Opulus, the snowball tree, is a general favourite, but tomentosum plicatum, Japanese snowball tree, is a choicer and more beautiful shrub. V. t. Mariesii is another distinguished member of this group. A rounded shrub of 6–8 ft. with its fish-bone branches densely clustered on their upper sides. with large cream-white flowers (bracts), it is exceedingly attractive as a lawn shrub in June. All these viburnums are content with normal garden conditions. Cuttings, rooted off-sets. No pruning required.

WISTARIA SINENSIS. The most beautiful of all climbing plants, this wistaria is recom-mended for the average garden where it is to be grown on a wall, though multijuga has larger racemes of more varied colours. W. sinensis does well and grows rapidly in a good loamy soil, and its 1-ft. violet-mauve, scented racemes are singularly lovely in late spring. Needs all possible sun. Layers.

YUCCA. These noble sword-leaved American shrubs of the lily order are invaluable for late summer flowering and look their best when associated with grassy-leaved plants or set-out in commanding positions in the formal garden. All raise enormous panicles of bell-like flowers, cream-white, often tinted with rose or green. One of the most imposing is Y. gloriosa, 6–8 ft., but filamentosa and recurvifolia are close-up in merit. Good loamy soil; full sun.

ZENOBIA PULVERULENTA. This southern U.S.A. 3-ft. shrub is easily the best of its kind. Its leaves are a frosty emerald with an infusion of rose, especially when young, and in June and July ½-in. bell-like flowers, white and waxen in texture, are carried in long spikes. Non-limy, cool soil. Cut back flowering ends to new wood soon as blooming ceases.

EUCRYPHIA GLUTINOSA

The most beautiful of summer-flowering shrubs, this distinguished Chilean grows erect to 12–18 ft. A prolific bloomer, the 2-in. bowl-shaped, satin-white flowers are very fragrant and filled with a mass of coral-tipped stamens. In the later autumn the rose-like leaves develop rich shades of orange-flame before falling. The shrub is quite hardy and thrives in a lime-free soil, light yet cool, plentifully supplied with humus. Seed.

CISTUS LADANIFERUS

PHILADELPHUS VOIE LACTEE

RHODODENDRON LODER'S WHITE

One of the best of all hybrid rhododendrons for the average garden, with a handsome, medium-sized leafage in a cheerful green and immense trusses of blossom in April or May. Opening from clear pink buds, the wide bell-shaped corollas, which mature to white, have wavy margins and the shrub is a free bloomer. Very hardy and accommodating, it thrives in any lime-free loam, with humus, and prefers light shade. Layers.

CLEMATIS LASURSTERN

This well-known variety is typical of the Patens section of spring-summer clematises. The 6–8-in. blue-lavender blossoms being borne in profusion on the older wood, pruning (March) is confined to a removal of the weak and dead branches only. Suitable for garden arches, walls or rambling over an old tree, preferably with the lower parts in shade. A good rich loam with plenty of crushed mortar is appreciated. Other fine varieties of this section are Edouard Defosse, Miss Bateman and Sir Garnet Wolseley.

MAGNOLIA CAMPBELLII

The most magnificent of its wonderful family, a tall tree of elegant build with moderately large leaves and (March) 8–10-in. flowers, heavily textured, fragrant and a warm rose-pink. Hardy and a good doer in an average loam, but takes 15–20 years to reach the flowering stage.   Most suitable for localities where spring frosts are infrequent.   Layers.

ABELIA FLORIBUNDA

THE OLD BLUSH CHINA ROSE

STYRAX JAPONICUS

One of the most beautiful of June-flowering trees, this makes an elegant standard of 12–15 ft. with a widespread mushroom head. The snow-white bells, which hang beneath the slender branches, are produced very luxuriantly and the tree is hardy and well content with any medium loam. No pruning required beyond occasional removal of congested branches.

PHILADELPHUS FANTAISIE

A hybrid mock orange which, being only 5–6 ft., is of interest to owners of small gardens. It is charming in summer, when the drooping branches are laden with saucer-shaped, $1\frac{1}{2}$-in. warm-white flowers (not too heavily scented) with rose-purple flush at the base. A good shrub for dry soils but will do anywhere in sun. Old wood and flowering ends may be cut out after flowering.

PRUNUS COMMUNIS

The common almond has won a wide esteem as a hardy, early-flowering tree with rose-pink flowers clustering its leafless branches. An appropriate tree for places of limited area and one that does remarkably well in town gardens. It is not particular as to soil and may be regarded as good and satisfactory under most conditions. There are several varieties, including one with larger flowers and a double.

VIBURNUM DAVIDII

SPIRÆA BRACTEATA

EUCRYPHIA CORDIFOLIA

An evergreen species and one of the choicest of all flowering trees, but will not stand very severe frost. The leathery, oval leaves are a rich green, and the bowl-shaped, fragrant blossoms, over 1 in. across, a firm white with a prominent boss of chocolate anthers. Since the flowering season covers September and October it has a special garden value, and whereas E. glutinosa must have an acid soil, this Valdivian does well on chalk or lime, but some humus is desirable.

PHILADELPHUS BURFORDIENSIS

A notable hybrid raised by the late Sir William Lawrence, this makes a bush of 6–8 ft. It is bold in leaf, and the flowers, single and 2 in. across, are snowy white with orange anthers. These flowers, only delicately scented, are borne in the utmost profusion, crowding the laterals of the previous year. A welcome addition to the mock oranges and one that will give no trouble under ordinary conditions. Cuttings or rooted off-sets.

ROMNEYA COULTERI

The Californian bush poppy, most beautiful of all soft-wooded shrubs, attains 6–7 ft.   Leaves and stems are grey-green, and the pure-white flowers, 5–6 in. across, deliciously fragrant and centred with a massive cluster of orange stamens, are borne in abundance from July onwards. Hardy in a light, well-drained soil.   Must have full sun.   Should be cut to the base in early April.   Root-cuttings, but suckers will often succeed if carefully lifted and nursed.

CISTUS GLAUCUS

HYDRANGEA PANICULATA

PRUNUS YEDOËNSIS

Making a 20-ft. widely spread tree, this is perhaps the best of the earlier single white Japanese cherries. A most reliable variety, blossoming with prodigal luxuriance (March and April) year after year, the 1-in. flowers being fragrant and delicately flushed with rose when first opened. The leaves are large and in autumn assume rich shades of orange and red. Makes a fine lawn standard. Is content with any free soil, limy or otherwise.

RHODODENDRON YUNNANENSE

An evergreen averaging 6–8 ft. of erect growth, this is one of the most useful and steadfast of rhododendrons. It is hardy and quite content in a free non-limy soil, with humus, preferably in light shade. The flowers, yielded profusely every season, usually in late May, are a lovely tint of silvery blush, but there are diversions in a thin bluish lilac or rosy mauve, all having a " flare " of red brown on the upper segment.

THE DOUBLE YELLOW BANKSIAN ROSE

EUCRYPHIA NYMANSAY

RHODODENDRON RACEMOSUM

MAGNOLIA PARVIFLORA

The most useful and beautiful of summer-flowering magnolias for general culture. A wide bush of 8–12 ft., it yields, from May to autumn, 4-in. saucer-shaped, waxen-white flowers, with a rose-crimson centre and richly scented. One of the easiest of magnolias, it will prosper in a normal loam and, beginning to flower when only 2–3 ft. high, continues season after season with unfailing luxuriance. Seed.

PHILADELPHUS BURKWOODII

RHODODENDRON WILLIAMSIANUM

PRUNUS COMMUNIS POLLARDII

RHODODENDRON MUCRONATUM

PIERIS FORMOSA

HYDRANGEA QUERCIFOLIA

This choice N. American shrub grows widely to some 4–6 ft. Its five- to seven-lobed leaves are large and a medium green, and the flower panicles, erect and up to 8 in. in length, are white changing to rose-purple as they slowly fade. The broad leaves also acquire good autumn tints. Quite reasonably hardy, the oak-leaved hydrangea will thrive under average garden conditions, with part shade in the south. Cuttings. No pruning required.

NEILLIA LONGIRACEMOSA

Allied to the spiræas, this Chinese shrub throws up gracefully arched golden-brown wands to 6–7 ft. The leaves are heart-shaped, often tinted with bronzy yellow, and it produces in June and July bright rose-pink flower racemes 4–6 in. long. The foliage sometimes colours well in autumn. An unusual and attractive shrub for a cool loam, preferably rather moist. The older wood should be thinned out occasionally just after flowering. Increased by off-sets.

HOHERIA LYALLII GLABRATA

The hoherias are not hardy, but they are well worth a place where winters are not too severe, and the above variety is one of the most trustworthy. It makes a tall shrub, or small tree, and the flowers it bears in July are over 1 in. across, shallow-cup-shaped, crystal-white and deliciously scented. Perhaps the finest of all New Zealand shrubs, this choice member of a distinguished family enjoys a free loam of average quality. No pruning required.

CLEMATIS MACROPETALA

DEUTZIA MAGICIAN

118

CARYOPTERIS CLANDONENSIS

One of the best hybrid shrubs of recent years, and much superior to the old C. Mastacanthus, one of its parents. It grows to about 2 ft. and makes a neatly rounded bush very suitable for a sunny mixed border. From late July to November it bristles with long flower spikes whorled with plumbago-blue blossoms. Quite tolerably hardy in a light soil. Only pruning required consists of cutting back spent flower stems in spring. Cuttings.

LEIOPHYLLUM BUXIFOLIUM

STRANVÆSIA DAVIDIANA

PIERIS JAPONICA

This charming evergreen is a bush of about 5–6 ft. with leathery, dark-green glossy leaves which are a glistening bronzy amber when young. The blossoms, carried in racemes of 4–6 in., are egg-shaped, white and sweet-scented, the stalks and calyces often tinted with red. Flowering in March and April, the blooms are apt to be frozen, hence a place beneath the branches of deciduous trees should be chosen. Thrives in a medium, lime-free loam with humus. Needs no pruning. Layers.

MAGNOLIA STELLATA

ROSE CELESTIAL

EXOCHORDA GIRALDII

One of the Chinese pearl-bushes and a beautiful hardy shrub for a coolish soil, or a well-drained place near water. Growing to 8 ft. or so with the grace of a willow, its young leaves are a rosy fawn, and these are soon followed in May by long and elegant racemes of pure-white flowers, slightly fragrant, and $1\frac{1}{2}$ in. across. Cut out dead or feeble wood when necessary. Rooted off-sets often obtainable, or may be raised from seed.

MAGNOLIA LENNEI

A beautiful hybrid of the highest garden merit, with very large leaves and an open, spreading habit, but of no great height. The massive goblet-shaped flowers are 4–5 in. each way, richly fragrant and white inside with a flush of crimson-purple on the exterior. These flowers, commencing after the spring frosts, are yielded May–June and at intervals during summer. Plants will begin flowering when only 3–4 ft. Needs a strong loam with plenty of humus. Best propagated by layering.

HERBACEOUS
AND MIXED BORDERS

Notes on the Cultivation and Arrangement
of Hardy Perennials

THE herbaceous border has long been a leading feature of our English gardens. That, in truth, is an underestimate of its position, for with many it has remained for generations the pride of the pleasance to both professionals and amateurs, the peak of the garden's achievement at the full of summer splendour. And so deeply has it become established in our horticultural round that, despite recent changes, it survives, and will continue to survive, as something typical of our traditional gardening aspirations.

The changes referred to have arisen largely through economic pressure. Orthodox herbaceous borders are costly to maintain, and as labour became more expensive and taxation increased, staffs and general upkeep had to be cut down. We had perforce to remodel our borders by going in for more permanent plants and those which need less cultural attention, even so far as to introduce shrubs. Thus the border underwent a transformation. It became a mixed border with a greatly decreased expenditure and a comparative freedom from care. But it was something more than this, for with the development of less formal and more natural gardens there arose the desire for an all-the-year-round interest. This the conventional herbaceous border could never give, but the mixed assembly provided it without stint, yielding us a never-failing fascination from January to December. But, even so, "the herbaceous," in much of its rich and stately dignity, is still with us and long will be. Modifications may have arisen to challenge its supremacy, they may have ousted it from the gardens of the many, but it prevails, the most triumphant note of the garden round.

In dealing with herbaceous plants and the treatment of them we must, in view of the above, take a broad view, regarding them as belonging to both the border of the professed lover of purely herbaceous and the blended lay-out. We do not overlook the fact that many herbaceous perennials are waterside and woodland dwellers and that the term herbaceous is commonly used to embrace certain evergreen plants and bulbs, and even biennials. The list of these given in the following pages is not intended to be comprehensive, but it has been compiled with the view to affording the general run of gardening folk a choice of the principal families and their varieties, with a few brief hints on cultural requirements. This choice will always be subject to one's individual taste. The nature of the garden must also be considered and the quality of the soil. Wherefore, it is only on general lines that we can proceed here.

If there are two essentials which must be observed in growing herbaceous plants, no matter where or how they are placed, one is thorough drainage and the other deep cultivation. Even bog plants dislike stagnant water, and, as for soil preparation, trenching always pays handsomely in affording a freer scope for root-action and as a means of warding off dryness in summer. In both sticky soils of a heavy nature and light gravelly mediums we have found fibrous or granulated moss-peat of the utmost value. It renders the former more friable and more easily worked, and with the thin and sandy (or gravelly) it provides a means of absorbing moisture and holding it. Vegetable compost, especially containing decayed leaves, is close up in value and may be worked into most soils during preliminary preparation and used for mulching. Mixed with moss-peat in about equal parts it forms an even better material for both the purposes named. Nor will anyone overlook the fact that by converting the trimmings and other refuse from borders to compost heap we shall be practising the very essence of economy and to a great extent rendering the border self-supporting.

In arrangement the herbaceous border, as in the case of the plants themselves, must be decided by the individual, his scope and conditions, but some definite planting plan must be conceived whereby the entire effect will be right and pleasing. Tall plants must, as a general rule, be to the rear of lesser ones, colours that "clash" must not be in proximity to one another, nor can dominant tints be permitted to overwhelm those of more tender hue. The occupants should be arranged in groups according to their kind, and it is an error to repeat a plant at regular intervals, this presenting a dotted and wearisome effect. Where one can afford to do so borders entirely composed of kindred colours, or a lay-out presenting a uniform colour sequence from the rich and brilliant to tints of melting, misty softness can be very beautiful. Then there are attractive possibilities in the way of seasonal borders of one class of plant, irises for June, Michaelmas daisies or dahlias for autumn. For our own part we deprecate too much uniformity in the border, all plants graduating evenly in height from front to back, as much as we deplore repetition and a spotty colour drift. Rather would we have the general front-to-rear pitch broken here and there by a deep bay of quite dwarf plants, and by bringing boldly forward to the front margin some well-chosen tall variety that will lend a strong note of character to the lay-out. Another thing to avoid is the mixing of such things as yuccas, montbretia, day-lilies, kniphofias and other narrow-leaved plants with those of broader leaf. Such as these should be segregated apart if we are to realise their full value and avoid loss of garden merit both in regard to themselves and their companions. But in any event we must let the border be our own, our own creation and our own joy, with an individuality that is intimate and persuasive.

So it is with the mixed lay-out of which we have spoken. Here arrangement is a much simpler matter once the shrubs are in, for these, holding the key positions, will be the first to be planted. Though informality must be our guiding star with these, a good general plan is to arrange the shrubs so that there will be irregular triangular or rounded beds at intervals between them. Then in these beds, with their sheltering walls of bushes, we can do as we will with such suitable candidates as lilies, pæonies, irises, anemones, evening primroses and columbines, not to mention autumn-spring bulbs and a foreground of such hardy easy-going rock plants as will provide a year-round interest. The number of plants that may appropriately accompany shrubs is so vast that none will be in any difficulty in making a choice to suit his or her particular fancy. But it will not be amiss to emphasise that discretion must always be exercised in our selecting, for it is an easy matter to create a false note. Why delphiniums should look all wrong in conjunction with rhododendrons, and why pæonies should be entirely right and sympathetic, we do not propose to decide. But we know such things are so and none of us can afford to remain unaware of them.

Another point that must be observed if we are to avoid unnecessary difficulty and expense, and at the same time reap the highest reward, is that of recognising the relationship of the plant to the soil. By choosing such things as will suit our conditions we are more than half-way to success. Just as the would-be grower of exhibition roses could not expect much in the way of results—at all events without a deal of labour and expense—unless he has a rose soil, so the enthusiast on Michaelmas daisies would be wise to turn to something else if he has got only a thin gravelly root-run to offer them. One can, it is admitted, do much—if we do not grudge the cost—with the madonna lily and bearded irises in a non-limy soil. But the way is a hundredfold easier and prospects infinitely brighter with such plants where lime naturally prevails. The choice in plants is so enormous, and there is something that will respond to soils of every description with a minimum of assistance from ourselves, that it is only courting trouble to attempt to proceed with subjects towards which one's conditions are hostile. Indulge in trial, in coaxing the wayward, in overcoming obstacles, by all means, but these diversions which whip our energies and further our interests must be incidental to, not the mainstay of, the garden as a whole. Provided we select our plants with discretion, and the more permanent they are the better, our mixed border, the very key-note of which is permanency, will prove to be not only a delight but a comfort and a refuge.

Turning for a moment to informal watersides and woodland perennials, the same rules apply with even greater force, for in such places we have a further reason for concentrating on permanent things—that of preserving the natural amenities of such places from all un-necessary cultivation. There are hosts of good plants that will flourish along with a reason-ably controlled native herbage, and it is among these that we will usually find those that in flower and foliage are most in accord with such environments. It is in view of the great increase in these informal phases of gardening that we have included in the following pages many plants especially adapted for such departures, and the brief notes accompanying these we hope and believe will be helpful to the many who are more or less new to a deeply engrossing and economic issue of our pursuit.

There is yet another way by which labour may be curtailed without any reduction in garden beauty, and that is by so covering the ground that summer moisture is retained and weeds smothered. To " have no patience with bare ground," to quote William Robinson, may not come within the policy of the many accustomed to a more leisured and less exacting age, but we are convinced that, as a solution of a large share of our troubles to-day, enveloping foliage, whether of the plants themselves or an undergrowth of dwarf creepers, provides a means of relief from much of the burden of maintenance.

It will be gathered from the foregoing that the bogy of border maintenance that has given most of us so much cause for anxiety can be disposed of by practical means which, rather than tending to depreciate garden value, actually enhances it by providing us with a year-round charm to which the old-time herbaceous border never aspired. This all-season interest means very much to any garden and, further, the more modern way of treating herbaceous plants enables us to appreciate them individually to an extent that was undreamed of a few decades ago. They may be grouped, of course, to an extent in keeping with the area, but each kind will remain as a unit, an individual, and it is our conviction that it is in this manner that we shall derive the keenest delight, the most engrossing satisfaction and the richest return from the garden in its entirety.

HERBACEOUS PLANTS

A List of the Most Worthy

ACHILLEA. A useful family of summer-blooming border plants, among the best of which are the yellow-flowered A. filipendulina, 4 ft.; millefolium, Cerise Queen, 2–3 ft.; and the double-white Ptarmica, The Pearl. Ordinary soil; sun; division.

ACONITUM. The monkshoods are a valuable race of late-flowering perennials, doing well in any border soil and remarkably ornamental when boldly grouped, as between moderate-sized shrubs. Best kinds are Wilsonii, bright powder-blue, with the more branching Barker's Variety in rosy azure, both 5–7 ft.; Fischeri (4 ft.), rich blue spires in autumn; Napellus Sparks' Variety, 5–6 ft., August; N. bicolor, blue and white; and lycoctonum, yellow. Division only when necessary.

ALLIUM. The ornamental garlics include many good spring–summer border plants in heights from 2 ft. to 5 ft., the flowers usually in a large umbel. Beesianum, harebell-blue; giganteum, rose-lilac; Moly, golden yellow; Rosenbachianum, rose-purple; and triquetrum (see p. 160) among the best. A medium, free loam; in groups between shrubs or in herbaceous border. Seed or division.

ALSTRŒMERIA. Hardy border plants of the highest merit for summer flowering. A. aurantiaca, yellow to orange-flame, 2–3 ft., most generally useful, but the newer and taller Ligtu hybrids—pink, yellow, orange and tangerine—should be noted. Plant at least 6 in. deep in groups. Moisture needed during growing period. Will do in light shade.

ALTHÆA ROSEA. The popular hollyhock revels in a good deep loam and is an invaluable plant for the back of the border. Propagated by seed (a sowing annually, for plant is short-lived), special varieties by spring cuttings or division. A great number of varieties in rich reds, purple, peach, rose, scarlet, yellow and white; singles and doubles. Imperator strain one of the finest.

ANAPHALIS TRIPLINERVIS. A pretty grey-leaved, white-flowered "everlasting," 18 in. Good drought resister and the August blossoms (useful for cutting) remain most of the winter. Light soil; sun; division (see p. 170).

ANCHUSA. Handsome perennials, notable for the brilliance of their blues. Highly ornamental in the border or between shrubs, especially varieties of A. italica, including the striking Dropmore, Morning Glory, Opal and Pride of Dover, 3–5 ft., May–July. A. sempervirens, 2–3 ft., and the early myosotidiflora, 18 in., both brilliant blues and charming for woodland or shady borders. The italica varieties need a good deep loam, freely drained. Root cuttings.

ANEMONE CORONARIA. The poppy anemones, singles and doubles, in a great variety of brilliant colours, are among the most popular of spring flowers, for they give masses of gorgeous blossom in the garden and are excellent for cutting. They will do in any average well-drained soil with full sun. Plant in succession from October to March. Lift tubers when foliage has died down and keep dry until planting time. Among the best strains, including stellatas, are the Caen, Nice, St. Bavo and St. Bridgid. Numerous varieties with colour descriptions to be found in any bulb list.

A. FULGENS. A wonderfully vivid windflower with dazzling scarlet flowers, single and double. Plant in autumn; well-drained, rich soil; sun. Will thrive even in turf in some gardens, capricious in others.

A. JAPONICA. One of the oldest and best of the taller windflowers and a first-rate autumn-flowering border and woodland plant. May be grouped in any free soil in sun or part shade. Average height, 2–3 ft. A selection of varieties should include Honore Joubert, Lady Ardilaun, Louis Uhink, whites; Queen Charlotte, Alice, Rosea elegantissima, Prince Henry, Margarita, pale blush to red-crimson. A. hupehensis, a later dwarf form with bright red flowers. Division in spring.

A. PULSATILLA. The pasque-flower is one of the loveliest of spring flowers, making lusty clumps of finely divided silky leaves and yielding in long succession large bell-shaped flowers on 8-in. stems. In colour these range from white through palest lavender to rosy mauve, purple, wine-crimson and maroon. Easy and long-lived in any decent loam, with sun. Division.

A. TRIFOLIA (see p. 172).

ANEMONOPSIS MACROPHYLLA. An elegant anemone-like plant of about 18 in. from Japan, with leaves suggesting a spiræa and nodding, waxen blossoms, white with violet markings, on long, slender stems. For a part-shaded border or woodland. Cool vegetable soil. Top-dress with compost in spring (see p. 164).

ANTHEMIS CUPANIANA. A useful front-row border plant, making a low mat of finely cut silver foliage and producing all summer large ox-eye daisies on 9-in. stems. Poor, stony soil; sun. Division.

A. SANCTA-JOHANNIS. The most ornamental of these camomiles and a choice plant for a sunny border of light soil. Grows to about 18 in., and over its fern-like leaves bears a succession of daisies in a glowing orange. Division; cuttings.

A. TINCTORIA. In the same way as the above but taller, rising to 3 ft. Several varieties in shades of golden yellow, Perry's, Roger Perry and Thora Perry being outstanding, with Buxton's Variety, a pale ivory-yellow. Easy culture. Division.

ANTHERICUM. The St. Bernard's and St. Bruno's lilies are graceful liliaceous plants of 2–3 ft. with snow-white flowers. They like a good but free soil, and are suitable for partly shaded borders or open woodland. Division of bulbs (autumn) or seed.

ANTHOLYZA. Showy plants from the Cape, allied to montbretia. Will make massive clumps with sword-like leaves and broad sprays of blossom (3 ft.) in late summer and autumn. A. æthiopica, red and yellow; A. crocosmioides, scarlet and orange, recommended. Rich but light soil, sharp drainage. Division of corms, early spring.

AQUILEGIA. The familiar columbine, one of the most ornamental of perennials, is best known in its long-spurred varieties, of which there are many fine strains in blue, rose, red, crimson, yellow and other colours. But the old and variable A. vulgaris in its best forms, such as Munstead White, is a worthy plant. While the latter are best adapted for woodland and shrub plantations, the long-spurs are admirable in herbaceous borders. All these columbines are hardy, good-natured plants under average conditions. Division. Among species the blue and white A. cœrulea of North America, the scarlet and gold formosa and the long-spurred golden-yellow longissima are worthy of special notice.

ARTEMISIA. A large genus of herbs or sub-shrubs notable for their aromatic foliage, which is usually silvery. A. Abrotanum (southernwood), one of the most fragrant, and A. canescens, making a wide 9-in. mat of silver filigree, perhaps the best for foliage. A. lactiflora, 5–6 ft., with white plumes like a spiræa, is effective if happily placed. Light soil. Division or cuttings.

ASTER. Hardy, handsome and easily managed under ordinary border conditions, the Michaelmas daisies constitute by far the major portion of our garden asters. They are indispensable in late summer and autumn. In stature, size of flower, colour and habits they offer an enormous selection of varieties. The principal sections are the Amellus, Novæ-angliæ and Novi-belgii. The amellus asters are large-flowered, average about 2 ft. and are permanent, seldom needing attention. The other two groups, of which Novi-belgii is the larger, comprise for the most part the tall Michaelmas daisies, but include several charming dwarfs. All good nursery lists include selections of varieties. In cultivation most of these, the amellus excepted, need periodical division and an annual top-dressing of compost in spring. Michaelmas daisies are most effective in masses and are well adapted for colour grouping.

A. ACRIS is a beautiful 2-ft. border plant of compact growth thronged with lavender-blue flowers in late summer, and A. Thomsonii crossed with A. Amellus has given us A. Frikartii (see p. 152) with the excellent variety, Wonder of Staffa. The new race of dwarf Michaelmas daisies, of which Marjorie (p. 46) and Remembrance (p. 169) are typical examples, offer several varieties of first-rate miniatures for the front of a sunny border. These are lowly and dense in growth, prodigious bloomers and take care of themselves indefinitely.

ASTILBE. The most ornamental of this beautiful family are the hybrids which, throughout the later summer, make a brave show with their elegant foliage and waving plumes (2–5 ft.) of blossom. Colour ranges from white to blush, pink, lilac, rose-red, salmon-red and ruby-crimson. Among the many notable varieties are Gertrude Brix, ruby-red; Gloria purpurea, deep rose; Granat (see p. 176); Rheinland, ruby-rose; Salmon Queen, warm pink; and the whites King Albert and Prof. V. D. Wielen. All these will thrive in any moist soil, with sun. Better for division every third or fourth year. Top-dress with compost in early spring.

A. SIMPLICIFOLIA HYBRIDA. A delightful plant with singularly graceful plumes of no more than 18 in. The latter are a rich warm pink, and there is a good white. An admirable plant for gardens that cannot accommodate the larger kinds, and as easily grown. May be propagated rapidly by division and is attractive singly or in groups. Will do with less moisture than the taller hybrids (see p. 154).

ASTRANTIA. Ornamental in a quiet way, the masterworts are attractive perennials for woodland or shady borders. They make a bushy growth of some 12–18 in. and raise above this umbels of blossom, usually in silver and green. The prettiest of the family is A. maxima (often called carniolica) with umbels of a soft chalky pink. Another good one is A. major (see p. 167). Any soil; division or seed.

BAPTISIA AUSTRALIS. A lupin-like plant of 2 ft., with a fresh green foliage and spikes of leadwort-blue pea-flowers. In a mixed border or collection of old-time flowers this always arouses interest. Moderately light and moist soil; sun; division.

BOCCONIA CORDATA. A handsome and robust perennial of the poppy order, with noble glaucous wavy-margined leaves and plumes of rosy-orange in summer. Will attain 6–8 ft. in good, loamy soil. Coral Plume, with redder panicles, a fine variety. B. microcarpa even taller, with rosy seed vessels, but inferior in general garden merit. Seed.

BORAGO. The true borages are few, but several anchusas are often called by their name. B. officinalis, a biennial, is a handsome 18-in. native, with raspy leaves in a frosty emerald and flights of brilliant blue flowers nearly all summer. Best left to naturalise about mixed borders and between shrubs. B. laxiflora is a perennial with a flat rosette of broad leaves and semi-trailing stems bearing azure bells the season through. Will naturalise like the above.

BRODIÆA. A family of charming North American liliaceous plants, very sparse of leaf but bearing fine umbels of star-shaped flowers. A selection should include the 6-in., violet grandiflora; laxa, purple and other colours, 1 ft.; the pale blue candida of same height; peduncularis, violet-purple, 1 ft. These are not fastidious, but like moisture in summer. Division of bulbs; seed. Plant (3 in. deep) in colonies.

BULBINELLA HOOKERI. This choice little New Zealander of the Lily order is quite hardy and a charming plant for a mixed border. From a tuft of grassy, bronze-green leaves it sends up many 12–18 in. spikes of golden starry blossoms in June, the dense racemes suggesting an asphodel or eremurus in miniature. Also known as Chrysobactron Hookeri. Light soil; sun. Seed or division.

BUPTHALMUM SPECIOSUM. A noble waterside or moist border herb raising a 4-ft. pyramid of large heart-shaped leaves over which in the late season it displays widely branching heads of dark-eyed, orange sunflowers. Hardy and permanent and needs no attention beyond occasional mulching. Seed or division.

CALTHA PALUSTRIS. Our native king-cup in its best forms is an ornamental waterside perennial, thriving without care in any moist soil or shallow water. Tyerman's is a choice variety and the double-flowered C. p. plena specially recommended. The white-flowered C. leptosepala is an unusual diversion and C. polypetala a giant replica of C. palustris. Massive in leaf and with golden blossoms up to 3 in. across, polypetala is an admirable plant for a waterside affording space for its yard-long trailers. Division.

CAMASSIA. American plants of the lily order offering several stately species and varieties. The 4-ft. Cusickii and Leichtlinii, with elegant spires of lavender, rosy-mauve, cream or white stars, are the best of the talls. C. esculenta, a pretty 2-ft. plant with blue-violet or silvery azure flower-heads suitable for a more close-up position. All these (May and June flowering) prosper in a cool to moist border. Division and seed.

CAMPANULA. The border campanulas comprise a large number of beautiful species and varieties, most of them easily grown under normal conditions, their main season being June–August. Propagation is simple by seed, cuttings or division. The more important include C. carpatica (see Rock Plants); celtidifolia (lactiflora), azure-blue or white, 5–7 ft. glomerata superba, royal purple, 2 ft.; grandis (latiloba), violet-blue or white, 2–3 ft.; latifolia macrantha, rich purple-blue or white, 3 ft.; Medium, the indispensable and popular Canterbury bell in many colours and forms; persicifolia, from white to medium blue, with semi-doubles, 3 ft.; best varieties: Fleur de Neige, double white; Pride of Exmouth, double blue; Telham Beauty, single powder-blue; pyramidalis, biennial, blue or white, 5 ft.; urticæfolia, blue-mauve, double and single, 3 ft., for woodland or shrub border.

CATANANCHE CŒRULEA. An old and esteemed border plant with grassy leaves and many tall slender stems each bearing a blue or blue-and-white (bicolor) blossom suggesting a cornflower. Any free border soil with sun. Seed or division.

CENTAUREA. These robust and hardy herbs are massive and large-leaved, with bold thistle-like heads in full summer and a height of 2–8 ft. C. babylonica, yellow, is the tallest; dealbata, a rosy pink; macrocephala, a good yellow. C. montana, the "perennial cornflower," is a fine rich blue, with a white, a rosy-red variety, rubra, and the sulphur-yellow, Lady Hastings.

CENTRANTHUS RUBER. The red valerian, in its best forms, the white and the deep ruby-red, is a fine thing for naturalising about old walls, ruins and cliffs. Rather too invasive with its seed for the border proper unless spent flower heads are promptly removed.

CHEIRANTHUS. In addition to the wallflowers referred to under Rock Plants, the rich orange varieties, Pamela Pershouse, Rufus and C. Allionii, should be noted, the last coming true from seed. Varieties of the common wallflower, so inestimable for beds, borders and early flowering under glass, are fully described in the seed lists.

CHELONE BARBATA COCCINEA. This cousin of the pentstemons is a handsome plant for a sunny border and is permanent in a light soil. From a leafy base it raises tapered spires of 2–3 ft. which are hung with tubular rosy-scarlet blossoms over a long period in summer. Seed, cuttings or division.

CHRYSANTHEMUM. The indoor florist's chrysanthemums are outside our province here, but readers may be referred to the many hardy border varieties, tall and short, offered by nurserymen, making a special note of the Korean strain, including a long list of lovely varieties in both rich and delicate pastel shades.

C. MAXIMUM. A valuable and popular tall border daisy with white flowers, singles and doubles, a rich green foliage and erect habit. There are both early summer and later varieties, some of the finest being Early Giant, Esther Read, Edward VII, Mayfield Giant and Mrs. Lothian Bell. Average soil, not too dry in summer. Occasional division of the clumps desirable.

C. RUBELLUM. This novelty is an excellent border chrysanthemum carrying on 2-ft. stems large single flowers in a delicate pink from June onwards. Several varieties, the rich rose-pink Clara Curtis being perhaps the best. Quite hardy and easy in a free loam. Division (see p. 146).

CIMICIFUGA. The bugbanes comprise a group of elegant herbs of 3-4 ft. with foliage like a spiræa and white or cream bottle-brush inflorescences in late summer and autumn. C. simplex, milk-white, with leaning racemes, is the most beautiful, but close up in merit are C. cordifolia (see p. 148), dahurica and racemosa. Woodland or shady shrub border plants. Moist vegetable soil. Seed or division.

COLCHICUM. Among autumn bloomers there are no more estimable plants for woodland and shrub plantations than the meadow saffrons. They are readily established in a good sound loam and enjoy retreats sheltered from wind, preferably with grass or other dwarf herbage to preserve their leafless blooms against soil splash. Plant early August, top of bulb 2 in. deep, and leave alone. The finest species is C. speciosum, the large chalice-shaped flowers in white, rose-carmine or ruby-red. Bornmulleri, rose-lilac and white, is a rival in merit, and byzantinum, soft rose, is very charming. C. autumnalis includes the rosy-mauve type, a white and a singularly beautiful double white. Also many attractive hybrids offered by bulb merchants.

COREOPSIS. Showy American plants, perennial and annual, for the foreground of sunny borders where they will provide a rich display of colour and, incidentally, prove useful for cutting. Select varieties are: C. auriculata superba, yellow with red markings; grandiflora, lanceolata and Perry's Double, yellow; rosea, pale pink. Raise yearly, or biennially, from seed sown in spring; set out seedlings in autumn. Average free soil.

CYNOGLOSSUM AMABILE. Perhaps the loveliest of the borageworts, a biennial, but well worth the trouble of annual sowing, for the branching 2-ft. stems carry a crop of intensely blue flowers over glaucous leaves nearly all summer, making a magnificent display when generously grouped. C. nervosum, a perennial, in a deep gentian-blue, is also worth noting. A light, free soil for both of these.

DAHLIA. This well-known and popular late-flowering plant needs neither description nor recommendation. Leading varieties of all sections are offered in spring nursery lists. Those who prefer species to garden-made hybrids will appreciate D. Merckii shown on p. 173.

DELPHINIUM. No garden of herbaceous plants is likely to omit those stalwart perennial larkspurs known as delphiniums, with their lofty columns of blossom. Though blues are the plant's strongest note, other colours—purple, rose, white and bicolors—are available, and all are readily grown in a well-manured soil with sun. There are hosts of varieties for everyone's taste and requirements—dwarfs (Belladonna) as well as talls. Increase effected by division, preferably in spring. A summer mulch and copious watering during growth are essential where good spikes are expected. Space talls at least 4 ft. and stake as growth proceeds. Take precautions against slugs, especially winter and spring.

DIANTHUS. This beautiful family, including carnations, border varieties and the alpines (see Rock Plants), comprises a vast assembly of extremely useful and charming summer-flowering perennials, many of them deliciously fragrant. Those pinks suitable for border culture are admirable plants for a light soil, preferably limy or containing old mortar. They need all possible sun and are readily increased by layers or cuttings. A selection should include those of the Allwoodii and Highland strains. White Ladies (improved Mrs. Sinkins); Grenadier, scarlet; Fire, salmon-red; the crimson, Emperor; Her Majesty, white; Gladys Cranfield, white and wine-red; Fettes Mount, rose; Red Knight, old rose and maroon;

and such old kinds as Donizetti, Inchmery, Painted Lady, Jane Austin, Old Crimson and Ruth Fischer.

DICENTRA SPECTABILIS. One of the most striking of old-time plants. Rising to 2 ft. or more, with rosy-glaucous, fern-like leaves of rare grace and delicacy, the stems terminate in racemes of large locket-shaped, pendulous flowers, bright rose-red and white, in June. Likes a good vegetable soil, or peaty mixture, in sun or light shade. D. eximea (12–18 in.), and the rather shorter formosa, both with similar foliage to above and purple flowers, excel as carpeting or colony plants for woodland or shrub plantations. All may be increased by division in autumn.

DIERAMA PULCHERRIMUM. A supremely graceful late-summer plant with arching 4–6-ft. wands tipped with swinging clusters of tubular flowers—white, rose, lilac, purple. Moist soil, well drained. Seed; sun. Plant in groups in spring.

DIGITALIS. Best perennial border foxgloves are the yellow D. ambigua, and D. lanata, ivory and lilac (see p. 151). In biennials, Munstead White and such strains as the Shirley are distinctly good. Light soil, part shade; woodland or shrub border. Seed.

DORONICUM. Handsome, early-flowering perennials with golden-yellow daisy-flowers on long stems. Good for cutting. D. austriacum, 18 in., and plantagineum excelsum, 2–3 ft., most generally useful. Division.

ECHINACEA. Another striking composite for late summer, 3–4 ft. Flowers large and substantial, rose, crimson, red and wine-crimson. Vars. Taplow Crimson, The King, Ballard's Improved and Moerheimii. Good loam; sun. Division; seed.

ECHINOPS. The globe thistles, with blue or white globular heads and handsome foliage, are striking 3–6-ft. late bloomers, doing in average border conditions. E. banaticus, giganteus, Ritro and ruthenicus are choice kinds. Division or root cuttings.

EREMURUS. Noble liliaceous plants raising flowery spires of 4–8 ft. May–July. Exceedingly ornamental in groups between shrubs or margin of woodland. Rich, well-cultivated soil; annual mulching with littery compost in autumn. Many fine varieties, including Bungei, yellow; Elwesianus, pink; himalaicus, white; robustus, flesh-pink; and Olgæ, lilac, dwarf and late.

ERIGERON. Allied to the asters, the border erigerons are at their highest garden value in the various hybrids (see p. 168).

ERYNGIUM. The sea-hollies, 2–3 ft., are decorative border plants and useful for cutting. Their spiny foliage, stems and bracts are glaucous or metallic blue, and the large thistle-like flowers range in colour from pale silvery blue to the deepest violet. Light, gritty soil; full sun. A choice should include E. amethystinum, giganteum, Oliverianum, violetta and Zabellii. Seed or root cuttings.

FRITILLARIA. Bulbous plants of the lily order, the old F. imperialis being the most imposing with its 2–3 ft. stems crowned by large yellow or red bells in April. F. Meleagris, 1 ft., with chequered bells in white and various shades of wine-purple, is delightful when naturalised under trees or about mixed borders. These flourish in any good soil; former prefers stiffish medium and lime.

FUNKIA (HOSTA). Also akin to the lilies, these have a highly decorative foliage and put up many 1–2-ft. spires of bells in white, mauve or lavender in late summer. A short list should include the glaucous-leaved Sieboldii and Fortunei, ovata and grandiflora. Deep moist loam, preferably in shade. No cultural attention required. Division.

GAILLARDIA. The hybrid gaillardias are highly coloured, large-flowered perennials of about 2 ft. which will bloom nearly all summer and give no trouble in a warm free soil with full sun. The wide-rayed daisy-flowers are for the most part some glowing shade of yellow, orange, red and crimson, many of them being rich yellow with zones of some deeper hue. Dazzler, Monarch and Grandiflora strains comprise some fine varieties. Division in spring, or cuttings.

GALEGA. Showy plants of the pea family presenting a sheaf of erect stems (3–5 ft.) with a pretty foliage and dense clusters of blossom in full summer. G. officinalis, lavender-blue, the best-known species, is well represented by the pure-white Niobe; the lilac-blue and white Lady Wilson; carnea, flesh-pink and blue, and white Duchess of Bedford. G. patula Hartlandii, bright blue and white, also outstanding. Any good border soil; sun. Seed or offsets.

GENTIANA ASCLEPIADEA. A true herbaceous gentian and a most estimable plant for woodland, shady borders or waterside. It presents erect or gracefully arched leafy stems of 18 in. to 3–4 ft., and these carry in autumn many pairs of tubular flowers as large as foxglove bells in white or some shade of blue from palest azure to deepest violet. Seed. Best left to naturalise where it will.

GERANIUM ARMENUM. The finest of the border cranesbills, 2–3 ft., with large vine-like leaves and branching sprays of velvety, ruby-crimson, jet-eyed flowers the size of half-a-crown at midsummer. Should be placed in a sunny bay between shrubs. Lift and divide every 3–4 years. Division (see p. 166).

G. GRANDIFLORUM. This carpeting cranesbill of 1 ft. is admirable when colonised under trees, in shady borders or between shrubs. Its fine bowl-shaped flowers are lavender-blue, but in its variety, Gravetye, these are larger and richer in colour (see Rock Plants).

G. IBERICUM. A species of about 15 in. with broad leaves which colour well in autumn and large blue-purple flowers. A taller and more ornamental plant is G. i. platypetalum with more downy foliage and finer flowers, rich violet-purple, in copious heads (see p. 146).

G. PRATENSE. The meadow cranesbill, much improved by selection and cultivation, now includes forms of 3–4 ft. which produce nearly all summer ample cup-shaped blossoms in a gentle blue, and there are some good whites. The smaller sylvaticum is allied to this, and of both there are some good old-world double varieties in various colours.

G. NEPALENSE (see p. 174). A striking Himalayan member of the sanguineum group, described under Rock Plants.

All the above will thrive in any ordinary soil in sun or part shade. Little cultural attention needed, but top-dressing with compost is helpful. Better in mixed borders than herbaceous lay-outs. Division. See also under Rock Plants.

GEUM. Showy border perennials with single or double richly coloured flowers on branching stems, the colours ranging from yellow to orange and scarlet. Among most noteworthy are Dolly North, Fire Opal, Lady Stratheden, Mrs. Bradshaw, Princess Juliana. Any good border soil, not too dry; sun. Division.

GLADIOLUS. The popular gladiolus will maintain a succession of blossom from June to October. The earlies (Byzantinus and Colvillei) include some lovely whites, bicolors and rich purples, and are excellent for cutting. Of the later bloomers, the large-flowered and primulinus hybrids, there is an endless choice of gorgeous varieties, of which the bulb lists give ample description. All these are easy, adaptable plants, the corms being set out in groups, March or April, and lifted and dried for winter keeping. A fairly light soil is desirable, with full sun.

GUNNERA. These gigantic foliage plants, with leaves up to 6 ft. across, only fitted for large spaces where they can revel in a deep and rich moist soil. G. scabra and G. mannicata much alike, but latter has the larger leaves. Flower spikes should be cut early when foliage effect is desired. Cover crowns with the faded leaves in autumn. Seed or division. G. magellanica is a rampant little carpeting species of only a few inches, useful for covering bare weedy places by waterside.

GYPSOPHILA. Charming border plants, giving with their multitude of small flowers a delicate lace-like effect. Permanent in a warm border of light soil. G. paniculata, so useful for cutting, a popular and well-tried kind, but Bristol Fairy (double) and the blush-white, Rosy Veil, should not be omitted. Seed or division.

HELENIUM. Showy American perennials of the sunflower class rising from 2 ft. to 6 ft. and bearing, late summer–autumn, magnificent heads of bloom in yellow, orange, crimson or bronze. Good doers under average conditions and most useful for cutting. Riverton varieties, The Bishop, Chipperfield Orange, Moerheim Beauty, July Sun and Baronin Linden among the best. Seed; cuttings.

HELIANTHUS. Vigorous and highly ornamental, single and double perennial sunflowers of North America, rising to 6 ft. in a rich, well-cultivated soil, and presenting a glorious mass of colour, late summer–autumn. Periodical division in spring advised. A choice should include Lodden Gold, Soleil d'Or, Monarch and Miss Willmott, golden-yellow; W. Dodd and H. G. Moon, late yellow.

HELIOPSIS. Another American composite of value for the average sunny border, rising to about 4 ft.; the flowers yellow to orange. B. Ladhams, incomparabilis, Orange King, Orange Rosette, patula and ziniæflora notable varieties.

HELLEBORUS CORSICUS. A handsome plant for woodland or shady border with a bold dark-green leafage and imposing heads (late winter) of emerald-green bowl-shaped flowers. Needs a deep firm loam and to be left alone. Height about 3 ft. with a wider spread. H. fœtidus is, in a smaller way, an attractive and ornamental herb for similar positions.

H. NIGER. The best known of the hellebores, the Christmas rose is indispensable in the winter garden, its large pure-white flowers (especially fine in the variety altifolius) being produced in profusion on established plants. Any shady corner, with a good soil and an autumn dressing of compost, will suit this fine old plant. Division, but resents disturbance.

H. ORIENTALIS. The Lenten roses, which prevail from January to May, are hybrids between this and other species. They are a most valuable race and offer a vast number of varieties with a great colour range—white, cream, rose, red, crimson, lilac and burgundy. Will thrive indefinitely in conditions suiting above. Should not be disturbed unnecessarily (see p. 153).

HEMEROCALLIS. The day lilies, few in species, are many in variety, the latter comprising some of the most decorative of all herbaceous plants for a moist, cool soil with sun. In height they may be anything from 1 ft. to 4 ft., the long strap-shaped leaves are very ornamental and the large lily-like flowers in various shades of yellow, orange, flame, apricot and tawny bronze are fragrant and freely borne, June–August. Included among the finest are Aureole, Dr. Regel, Flame, fulva, George Yeld, Margaret Perry, Radiant and Sir M. Foster. Division.

HESPERIS. Charming old plants for mixed borders, shrub plantations or wild garden, with 3–4 ft. stems topped with lilac or white fragrant blossoms, June–August. The Scotch double rockets are general favourites with lovers of old-fashioned flowers, their stock-like heads, 12–18 in., being sweet-scented. Former easily maintained by seed, latter by cuttings, and these doubles need a rather stiffer and better soil and frequent change of ground.

HEUCHERA. Though often seen about rock gardens, heucheras are more suited to the border where, in a good average soil, they will throw up their elegant flowering sprays to 2–3 ft. They have prettily lobed, geranium-like leaves and respond to division. A good selection is provided by the H. sanguineum hybrids, viz. Gaiety, coral-scarlet; Oakington Jewel, coppery red; Pink Delight, bright old rose; Huntsman, a good red; Snow Flake, white; Pluie de Feu, scarlet; Red Pimpernel and the scarlet Shirley.

INCARVILLEA. In a warm, deep soil, with sun, the trumpet-flowers will make a brave show at midsummer and prove quite permanent and carefree. In height they vary from the 6 in. or so of I. grandiflora to the 18 in. or 2 ft. of I. g. brevipes, Bees' Pink and Delavayi. The flowers, gloxinia-shaped and very large, in colour run from pink to rose, crimson and crimson-purple.

INULA. Composites for sunny quarters in good, rather moist soil, the bold daisy-flowers being yellow or orange. The 12-in. I. ensifolia is a cheerful front row plant; Oculi-Christi, a little taller. I. Royleana and glandulosa, both 2 ft., are perhaps the finest of the talls for border work, the 6-ft. I. Helenium for woodland or wild. Seed or division.

IRIS BARBATA. The bearded iris has long been in high favour among herbaceous plants, its willing disposition and stately beauty winning favour with gardeners of all classes. Needs a drier soil than most, is fond of lime and at its best in spacious drifts. May be grouped in three sections—Dwarfs, March–May; May-flowering, about 2 ft.; June-flowering, 2–4 ft. There are legions of named varieties, of which the lists give full description. The planting of beardeds should be carried out July or August, the rhizomes on the surface and all made firm. Occasional dressings of lime advised for acid soils. Division, late summer.

I. KAEMPFERI. Perhaps the most magnificent of all irises, with flowers, in a wide variety of colours, 8–10 in. across (July–August). Enjoys a rich moist soil (preferably dry in winter) with a spring mulch of farm manure. Does best on a raised waterside. If grown in border, work in peat and leaf soil to retain moisture. A sun lover, provided roots kept damp in summer, but cannot endure lime (see p. 170).

I. LÆVIGATA. One of the loveliest of all irises and at its best in shallow water. Flowers blue with a gold streak, or white; varieties, Rose Queen and alba. Allied to the foregoing but less exacting, provided it has sufficient moisture. Height about 2 ft. Seed and division.

I. SIBIRICA. A singularly stately iris for border or waterside, making large tufts of grassy foliage and thrusting up a sheaf of 2–4-ft. stems, bearing in late May and June a succession of flowers in blue, violet, purple or white. One of the most accommodating of all irises, and orientalis, much like it with larger flowers, is equally easy. Many named varieties. Also of sibirica section is the tall, moisture-loving, violet-blue Delavayi, chrysographes, velvety wine-crimson; Wilsonii and Forrestii, both yellow. Seed of division (see p. 172).

I. TENAX (see p. 165) may be regarded as typical of the many charming little irises of the Californian section, including the lavender to purple I. Douglasiana, the white and yellow tenuis, the ivory-yellow bracteata and creamy-yellow Purdyi. All these are dwarf (9–18 in.) sun-lovers which revel in a light, free soil. Seed or division.

I. VERSICOLOR. The American form of our common flag iris, but a better garden plant. Delights in a wet soil and puts up many 2-ft. flowering stems (June–July) bearing blue-purple blossoms with varieties in clear blue and deep purple. Division.

Note: With the exception of the beardeds, most irises are divided, or moved most successfully, in spring when growth is active. Seed may be sown in open-ground beds in autumn, or in boxes exposed to frost and brought in in February.

KIRENGESHOMA PALMATA. A noble Japanese herbaceous perennial, ornamental both in foliage and flower. The broad, vine-like leaves on erect growths of about 2 ft. are a fresh green and in autumn they are topped by loose sprays of ivory-yellow flowers the shape of a shuttlecock. Needs a fairly moist soil, with humus, and should not be exposed to spring frosts. Careful division.

KNIPHOFIA. The poker plants have long been esteemed as late summer–autumn perennials of noble growth, flaunting a striking display of their tall fiery torches in some shade of yellow or scarlet. More recently many dwarf kinds have been introduced, these commencing early in summer and continuing until autumn. Not entirely frostproof but usually reliable in well-drained soil. Their best positions are margins of woodland or mixed borders. Spring planting recommended. Among the talls, Lord Roberts, Mt. Etna (The Rocket), Dr. Legate, caulescens and Northiæ are outstanding. In dwarfer varieties, Macowani, Goldelse, Rufa and corallina, recommended, with the brilliant scarlet, late-flowering Nelsonii as the choicest of the smaller species. Division in spring.

LAMIUM ORVALA. One of the few dead nettles which merit a place in the garden, and it is more suited to semi-wild spots than the border. But its white variety, L.O. alba, is a charming plant, well earning a place among shrubs or in shady borders. Its 18-in. growths are whorled with large creamy-white blossoms (May–June), and it comes true from seed, often raising its own offspring.

LATHYRUS LATIFOLIUS. The everlasting pea is an old favourite, notable for its willing disposition under any conditions, and attractive when rambling over a shrub or paling. Pink Beauty and Rose Queen are good colour varieties and The Pearl, a singularly beautiful white. Division, seed.

LEUCOJUM (see p. 171).

LILIUM. Perhaps the most beautiful of all flowering plants, the lilies combine stateliness, fragrance and grace with both brilliant and delicate colouring. Most of them happiest among lowly shrubs in a free, non-limy soil—save in the case of L. candidum and Henryi, which are lime-lovers—and all need good cultivation, generous feeding, below and on the surface, and perfect drainage. Propagation by seed, off-sets (bulbs), bulbils or scales.

From a great number of species, varieties and hybrids we select a dozen of all-round merit: L. auratum platyphyllum, 5–6 ft., white, crimson freckling, golden bar, August; Brownii (see p. 163); canadense, 3–4 ft., orange-red or yellow bell-shaped flowers; candidum, the well-known madonna, of which the Salonika form will often succeed where the type does not; chalcedonicum, 3–4 ft., brilliant scarlet turk's-caps, var. maculatum recommended; Hansonii, 4 ft., orange-yellow; Henryi, 6–7 ft., orange, August; Martagon, 4–6 ft., the white and black-purple var. dalmaticum perhaps the best; regale, 3–5 ft., white inside, wine-coloured without, golden glow at inner base of trumpet; speciosum (see p. 175); superbum, 8–10 ft., moisture-loving, bell-shaped flowers, orange with black specks; tigrinum, 4–6 ft., orange-flame, August–September, var. Fortunei giganteum the finest. All June–July flowering save where otherwise stated.

LUPINS. The lupin family is dominated by the L. polyphyllus varieties. These tall and massive perennials are first-rate herbaceous plants for a deeply worked medium loam and exceedingly showy in June and July with their towering spires closely set with pea-flowers in an endless variety of brilliant as well as delicate colours. Many fine strains, most noteworthy being the Russell. Seed; special colour forms by division.

LYCHNIS CHALCEDONICA. A striking old-time border plant of 3 ft. with broad heads of brilliant scarlet. L. coronaria, 2 ft., silver-grey foliage and rose-carmine flowers; L. viscaria splendens fl. pl., 15 in., with stock-like trusses of vivid rose-crimson. The Arkwrightii Hybrids also recommended. Easily grown in any free soil.

LYSICHITON (see p. 156).

LYSIMACHIA CLETHROIDES. A stately woodland, waterside or moist mixed border perennial with curiously bent white spikes (late summer) over leafy stems of 18 in. which develop fine autumn tints (see p. 166). Among others for similar positions are the golden-yellow L. punctata and Ephemerum with glaucous leaves and spires of cool lilac. Division.

LYTHRUM SALICARIA. The loosestrifes of the salicaria group are useful plants for late blooming by the waterside where they will follow the astilbes and spiræas with their gay racemes, rose or rose-crimson, on erect stems of 3–4 ft. Brightness, Lady Sackville and The Beacon (see p. 155) make a choice trio. Any moist soil. Division.

MECONOPSIS BETONICIFOLIA (BAILEYI) (see p. 157).

M. CAMBRICA. A delightful easy-going perennial poppywort for shrub borders and woodland with lemon-yellow flowers. Still better is the single orange (of which there is a double) with larger flowers on 18-in. stems all summer. Seed.

M. INTEGRIFOLIA. One of the choicest, making an 8-in. tuft of downy, strap-shaped leaves over which are poised immense saucer-shaped blossoms in a clear yellow. Moderately light, cool vegetable soil, part shade. Biennial. Seed (see p. 174).

Other meconopses of great charm and highly ornamental are nepalensis (Wallichi), 4 ft., pale blue, mauve, red or white; quintuplinervia, with nodding bells of harebell blue; regia, 4–5 ft., yellow; latifolia, 2 ft., sky-blue, for a dryish place; others treated like integrifolia. All biennial except quintuplinervia.

MIMULUS. The finest of the monkey-flowers for borders is M. Bartonianus, rose and yellow, and its scarlet variety, Sunset, 2–3 ft. For waterside and moist ground many brilliantly coloured varieties and hybrids of M. luteus. Cuttings and seed.

MONARDA DIDYMA. A grand old border plant of 2 ft. with fragrant foliage and heads of glowing scarlet flowers in late summer. Also purple, rose and white varieties. Ordinary soil; sun. Seed or division.

MONTBRETIA. Invaluable late summer and autumn bloomers, giving a glorious display of blossom in yellow, orange, flame, scarlet and vermilion. The older sorts, sound perennials in light soil, but the newer, large-flowered Earlham varieties need winter protection, or may be lifted, dried and started indoors early spring. Division of corms.

MORINA LONGIFOLIA. A stately old-time plant for a mixed border of average soil. From a bold tuft of spiny acanthus-like leaves it raises a 3–4 ft. spire which nearly all summer maintains a succession of rose to white blossoms in whorls. Hardy and permanent. Seed.

NOMOCHARIS PARDANTHINA (see p. 149).

ŒNOTHERA. The most beautiful evening primrose is Œ. biennis Lamarckiana, a biennial, 4–5 ft., but odorata and its variety, sulphurea, 3 ft., are close up. Œ. fruticosa, perennial, with a 2–3-ft. sheaf of stems crowned by masses of rich golden yellow, an excellent border plant of several varieties. Smaller, tufted or trailing species, with large flowers, white or yellow: missouriensis, eximia, triloba. All fragrant. Dry, warm soil, in sun. Seed; fruticosa by division.

ORCHIS FOLIOSA (see p. 147).

OSTROWSKYA MAGNIFICA. A singularly handsome 4-ft. cousin of the bellflowers, suggesting a magnified platycodon (q.v.), the white flowers, sheened with blue, being 4–6 in. across. Raise from seed and plant out 2-year seedlings in good soil cultivated to a depth of at least 2 ft.

PÆONIA. One of the oldest and most esteemed of border plants, with a great number of varieties in rich colours, doubles and singles, from May onwards. Finest species: P. Mlokosewitschii (see p. 154); the scarlet lobata and officinalis, rose, crimson, purple or white; Wittmanniana, ivory-yellow. Of officinalis a vast number of forms, and still more of the Chinese sweet-scented class, latter perhaps the best for average gardens. Deep, well-cultivated loam. Annual winter mulch of compost and manure. Division in early autumn or spring.

PAPAVER. The most beautiful of the dwarfer poppies is P. nudicaule, the Iceland, such strains as Gartref, Kelmscot and Sandford's having very large flowers on long stems in a most brilliant assortment of colours. Will thrive in any medium to light soil with sun; seed.

The oriental poppies, long-lived perennials for a deep, loamy soil, are magnificent border plants, with large blossoms in many gorgeous shades of red and crimson and more delicate tones of apricot, salmon and rose. Numerous varieties. Division in autumn. P. somniferum is a stately border biennial with a height of 3 ft., glaucous foliage and large single and double flowers in a wide assortment of striking colours.

PENTSTEMON. The hybrids are indispensable border plants for the later season, producing on 2–4-ft. stems long spires of tubular flowers in many colours, both brilliant and restrained. Not quite hardy, but raised easily by cuttings, may be wintered in frames and set out in May. A light soil with full sun. Should be grown in groups of distinct varieties.

PHLOX. Most important section is P. decussata, 2–3 ft., the many varieties of which, large-flowered, prolific bloomers, in a rich selection of gold and refined colours, will yield a brave display in the later season. A most useful phlox for preceding the above is P. Arendsii, comprising several choice, free-flowering varieties of 18 in. Good medium soil, well culti- vated. Top-dress (spring) with compost and manure. Cuttings in spring.

PHYSOSTEGIA. The " Obedient Plant " is a showy perennial and easy-going in any soil not too dry. At its best in P. virginiana, 2–3 ft. with heads of tubular blossoms in summer, pink, purple and white. P. v. speciosa Vivid, rose pink, an outstanding variety, good for cutting. Division.

PLATYCODON GRANDIFLORUM. This beautiful relation of the bellflowers puts up leafy 18-in. stems and crowns them in full summer with 2–3 in. bowl-shaped blossoms, in some shade of blue-purple to white, which break from balloon-like buds. P. g. Mariesii, a very choice dwarfer variety. Any deep, well-drained soil, liberally enriched. Best raised from seed and arranged in groups of self-colours. (See p. 164.)

POLEMONIUM. An attractive family of several species, mostly American. The erect stems ascend to 1–2 ft. and carry heads of cup-shaped, usually blue or white flowers in succession. Most reliable kinds, doing in any soil: P. carneum (see p. 161), cœruleum, humile and reptans. Division; seed.

POLYGONATUM. The solomon's seals are indispensable woodland and shady border plants. Exceedingly graceful and not too invasive, they are very effective in colonies and both permanent and care-free in any average soil. P. latifolium one of the finest, 3–4 ft., with broader leaves than the commoner P. multiflorum. Foliage and stature improved by winter mulching. Division.

POTENTILLA. The border cinquefoils offer several plants of value, notably P. nepalensis, cerise, and its variety Roxana, salmon-buff; atro-sanguinea, blood-red; Gibson's Scarlet; rupestris, white; recta, yellow. Heights from 18 in. to 24 in., pretty foliage and willing to do anywhere and flower all summer. Seed or division.

PRIMULA. Most of the border primulas delight in a cool soil, well enriched, light shade. Planted in drifts of single kinds most beautiful effects may be realised, and those mentioned below can be trusted to carry on for two or three years, when they should be divided or replaced by seedlings. Among the tall candelabra group, rising to 3–4 ft., following recommended: Aileen Aroon, orange-scarlet; Bartley strain, lovely shades of pink and rose; Beesiana, violet; Bulleyana, orange; helodoxa, late yellow; japonica, crimson, tawny-red or white; Lissadel Hybrids, "art shades"; pulverulenta, crimson. Others of outstanding merit are P. denticulata, early, blue-purple, ruby-crimson, white; Florindæ, late, yellow; Sieboldii, white to lilac and rose; sikkimensis, yellow. For spring flowering at border front, or for bedding, the common primrose offers many richly coloured varieties, white, crimson, purple and blue. P. Juliæ (see Rock Plants, also p. 150) invaluable for same purposes, as are the polyanthuses, of which there are many fine strains—Dr. Watts' gold-laced, Ipswich, Munstead and Spetchley. The old-world double primroses, always so popular, include many choice varieties, notably Lilacina, Dumoulin, Marie Crousse, Cloth of Gold (see p. 150), double white Bon Accord, Mme. Pompadour, sanguinea plena. Most primulas easily raised from seed or increased by division, autumn or spring.

PYRETHRUM ROSEA. The parent plant of the many varieties of the popular border varieties which are so good for cutting. Both singles and doubles in an extensive choice of fine colours. Average border soil. Best planted when growth has started in spring. Increased by division in July before second growth begins. Will yield autumn crop of flowers if earlier ones are promptly cut back.

RANUNCULUS ACONITIFOLIUS. Handsome perennial of 2 ft. for shady border. Its "major" form the best, but the double variety (Fair Maids of France) is a charming old-world plant; all white flowers. Few other buttercups of much border value, but R. Kerneri, 2–3 ft., has fine yellow blooms, and R. gramineus is a slender pretty plant with glaucous leaves and golden buttercups for a cool soil. Division.

RHEUM PALMATUM. The ornamental rhubarbs are highly attractive when associated with other large-leaved plants, their massive foliage being surmounted in summer by towering spires of blossom. R. Emodi, tanguticum and nobile are all good sorts, but we would give first choice to R. palmatum atrosanguineum, its immense, bronzy-green leaves, with red underparts and 6–8 ft. rosy inflorescences being extremely handsome. All these need a deep rich soil, with abundant moisture, spring–summer. Heavy winter mulching beneficial. Division.

RODGERSIA. Primarily waterside foliage plants, making massive clumps of handsome leafage, above which rise in summer tall spires or foamy panicles of white or rosy blossoms. Finest species are R. æsculifolia, pinnata and podophylla with bronze-tinted divided foliage, and tabularis with pale green round leaves up to 2 ft. across. Rich, deep, moist soil. Division.

RUDBECKIA. American composites of high border merit from July to October, the yellow or orange rays being centred by a prominent dark purple to black cone; also bronze and copper strains. Autumn Glory, Golden Glow and macrantha, 6 ft., a splendid trio of talls. In lesser heights, maxima, californica and the 2-ft. speciosa recommended. For purple varieties see Echinacea. Average border soil; sun. Division; seed.

SALVIA. Includes many summer-autumn border plants of value for light soils and genial climates, average height 2–3 ft. A selection should include S. azurea grandiflora, deep blue;

dichroa, blue and white; pratensis, violet; Sclarea, blue and white; turkestanica, lilac bracts and pale rose blossoms; uliginosa, vivid blue, late. S. splendens, scarlet, salmon, rose, and S. patens, lovely gentian-blue, only for mildest localities, or to be treated as half-hardy bedders. Two last increased by cuttings or division of tubers; hardier kinds, seed or division.

SCABIOSA. Large proportion of garden scabious are biennials, and of these there is an unlimited number of varieties, dwarf and tall, in many fine colours. Best perennial is the well-known S. caucasica, a long-season bloomer, admirable for cutting and with very wide flowers in white, lilac, lavender, blue and violet. Others worth noting are the violet-blue Fischeri and crimson lyriophylla. Free soil; sun. Division; seed.

SCHIZOSTYLIS COCCINEA. The grassy-leaved kaffir-lily is a most attractive autumn bloomer with 20-in. spires of scarlet flowers, excellent for cutting. Also a beautiful satiny-rose variety, Mrs. Hegarty. Moist, freely drained soil. Lift and divide every 2–3 years in spring.

SEDUM SPECTABILE. An erect plant of 20 in. with fleshy glaucous leaves and wide crests of blossom in a chalky rose-purple. Variety atropurpurea has flowers a deeper colour and bronzy foliage. Very effective, August onwards, and easy in a moderately moist soil. Division.

SIDALCEA. Valuable plants of moderate height for any soil with sunny aspect, with erect flowering stems bearing mallow-like blooms throughout the later summer in colours ranging from white through satiny pink to crimson, scarlet and ruby-red. Division.

SOLIDAGO. The American golden-rods also good late border perennials enjoying a well-cultivated soil, not too dry. Flowers yellow in feathery sprays. Heights run from 1 ft. to 6 ft. Golden Wings, Goldschleir, rugosa, Ballardii. Division; seed.

SPIRÆA ARUNCUS. A magnificent perennial for waterside, woodland or moist shady border, raising summer growths of 5–7 ft., topped by large foamy panicles, creamy-white. For small spaces the cut-leaved variety, Kneiffii, recommended. No cultural aid needed in good soil. Off-sets; seed.

S. PALMATA. A very beautiful, rich, moist-soil perennial of about 2 ft. with handsome leafage and crests of brilliant ruby-crimson in late summer. Also a white that is worthy of it. Allied is the equally vivid venusta, much taller, and the enormous gigantea towering to 8–10 ft. with white or rosy corymbs. All enjoy good living, and full sun if enough moisture. Division.

THALICTRUM. The meadowrue family contains some stately moist border plants, of which the late-flowering T. dipterocarpum, violet or white, is the most ornamental, its double variety (Hewitt's) being especially lovely. Height 6-8 ft. To be liberally grouped. Earlier bloomers of lesser stature and fine foliage are T. aquilegifolium, lilac-rose or white, and glaucum, yellow. Seed or division.

TRADESCANTIA. The old-world spiderworts very desirable border plants, prospering without care. Above 1-ft. tufts of grassy leaves they bear three-parted blossoms over a long period in many shades of rose, blue, lilac and purple. A select few should include Leonora, deepest blue; J. C. Weguelin, azure; J. Stratton, mauve; Taplow Crimson.

TRILLIUM. One of the best of American plants and long cultivated in our woodlands and mixed borders. T. grandiflorum, 9 in., with white flowers perhaps the best, but sessile (see p. 162), white to rose or red, rather taller, and the 6-in. white ovatum, are no less charming. They like a moist vegetable soil and light shade. Plant in groups, autumn, and leave undisturbed.

TROLLIUS. The globe-flowers, T. asiaticus, europæus, Ledebourii and others, have been merged into a host of hybrids which are excellent waterside or moist border plants, their prevailing colours being from golden-yellow to orange-flame, with heights of 2–4 ft. Foliage is attractive and they are prolific bloomers, mostly early summer. A free soil, generous cultivation and no lack of moisture main requirements. Division or off-sets. Among finest are Commander-in-Chief, orange; Earliest of All, yellow; Gold Quelle, orange-yellow; Golden Queen; Orange Globe.

TROPÆOLUM. The common " nasturtium," so useful as an annual—climbing or bedding—has some distinguished relations, notable among which are T. polyphyllum, a silver-leaved, orange-flowered trailer for a free soil in sun at the border front. This is quite hardy and permanent. Leichtlinii a dwarfer variety with a warmer colour. T. tuberosum is a pretty climber of about 4 ft., with red and yellow flowers, and T. speciosum is the finest of all, with its long ropes of scarlet draping a wall or festooning an evergreen bush. A cool peaty soil for this last, and it prefers a N. or E. aspect. Plant the roots in spring, 8 in. deep, and water following summer. Seed.

VERBASCUM. Tall and stately perennials or biennials of much ornamental value for shrub borders and margins of woodland, many of them with handsome foliage, silvery as well as green. Ordinary soil. Many will produce their own seedlings. Among the most ornamental are Broussa, white foliage, yellow, 5 ft.; nigrum, yellow or white, 3 ft.; olympicum, yellow, 6 ft.; pannosum, pale yellow, woolly leaves, 6 ft.; phœniceum, dwarf, purple, violet, rose, white. In hybrids, Pink Domino, Cotswold Beauty, Miss Willmott, New Departure.

VERBENA. Mostly summer bedding plants, of which there are many fine strains in a rich assortment of brilliant colours. The best border verbena is V. bonariensis, a South American species with 4–5 ft. rigid, branching stems topped by scabious-like flowers, crimson-purple, throughout later season. Should be generously grouped. Seed.

VERONICA. The border speedwells (later summer) should include V. exaltata, pale blue (Hatton's Var.) and white, 3–4 ft.; longifolia, lavender, and l. subsessilis, violet, 3 ft.; spicata, Blue Peter, Royal Blue, 2 ft.; virginica, white or lavender-blue, 4 ft. Average soil; sun. Division; seed.

VINCA. The periwinkles are soft-wooded shrubs, but included here for convenience. Admirable plants for sunless places, undercropping woodland trees, draping banks and covering areas of poor soil. V. major, most generally useful, but the autumn–spring V. difformis (see p. 145) worthy of wider recognition, and V. minor, in many colour forms, double and single, an even better and closer carpeter than either of above. All increased by runners.

VINCA DIFFORMIS

A charming autumn-winter-flowering periwinkle with much the same habit as the familiar V. major, but less invasive. The type has starch-white flowers in autumn and early winter, those of spring developing a pale lavender-blue tint. Also slate-blue and purple forms which are less hardy. A valuable plant for growing under trees and in shady borders, prospering in the poorest of stony or rooty soil. No cultural attention needed, but better for being cut down after flowering. Division or rooted runners.

CHRYSANTHEMUM RUBELLUM

GERANIUM IBERICUM PLATYPETALUM

146

ORCHIS FOLIOSA

The handsomest of all terrestrial orchids, this Madeiran is magnificent in a group, its massive cylindrical flower spikes, held erect on leafy stems of 20 in. in early summer, being a rich and velvety wine-crimson. A hardy plant and not at all difficult in a cool, but well-drained, gritty soil liberally treated with leafy compost, and this latter may be used as a mulch in early spring. Light shade is desirable and propagation may be carried out by seed or division, November or March. Best time to plant is early autumn.

CIMICIFUGA CORDIFOLIA

A stately woodland or shady shrub border herb of 4–5 ft. with erect stems furnished with broad, daintily cut leaves. Above these in full summer are tapering spires of white flowers in long succession. Deep soil, rather moist but well-drained. Can be raised from seed or by division. For other choice cimicifugas see Plant List.

NOMOCHARIS PARDANTHINA

One of the most beautiful of all liliaceous plants and the easiest and most trustworthy of its lovely race. It puts up erect stems of 18–24 in. or more, each bearing at its summit (June–July) several drooping bell-shaped flowers 2–3 in. across, in an exquisite rose-pink with a purple eye and frecklings within. A gritty, well-drained loam freely intermixed with leaf compost in light shade. Best raised from seed sown as soon as ripe.

PRIMULA JULIÆ

PRIMROSE CLOTH OF GOLD

DIGITALIS LANATA

An unusual foxglove that always strikes an interesting note in the shrub border or margin of woodland. The strap-shaped leaves and 18-in. flowering stems are densely coated with down, and the drooping tubular flowers (summer) are ivory-white with purple markings. A hardy but not long-lived plant. Very easily raised from seed, or may be left to produce its own self-sown offspring.

ASTER FRIKARTII

A hybrid between A. Thompsonii and A. Amellus and a most valuable plant. It comes into bloom much earlier than the general run of Michaelmas daisies, it is a sound perennial that never needs any cultural attention and its sturdy growths of about 2 ft. need no staking. Flowers are 2–3 in. across and yielded abundantly throughout the season. In addition to the typical violet-blue, such varieties as Wonder of Staffa, lavender-blue ; Jungfrau, lilac ; and Eiger, mauve, are noteworthy. Medium soil. Cuttings.

A HYBRID HELLEBORE

The Lenten roses follow the Christmas roses in the early year with a 3–4 months' succession of flowers in many shades of red, purple, mauve, lilac, rose, pink, blush, ivory and white. They make lusty clumps of 12–18 in. with decorative foliage, and thrive in a deep moist loam with part shade. No cultural aid is needed, but an autumn mulch of vegetable compost is helpful. Planting best done in September. Can be increased by division, but established plants resent disturbance.

PÆONIA MLOKOSEWITSCHI

ASTILBE SIMPLICIFOLIA HYBRIDA

LYTHRUM THE BEACON

The purple loosestrifes are highly ornamental waterside or moist border plants and valuable in providing colour in autumn. One of the most striking is the new variety, The Beacon, with rigid, erect, freely branched stems of 4 ft. and spikes of rose-crimson blossoms. No special culture required in a good soil. Increased by detaching rooted off-sets. Other varieties are noted in the Plant List.

LYSICHITON AMERICANUM

A hardy North-west American arum for waterside, shallow water or bog. The large butter-yellow spathes are thrust up in March and April and followed by enormous cabbage-green leaves which are decorative all summer. Deep soil essential. Can be raised from seed sown fresh, and will naturalise under congenial conditions. Prefers full sun, but does well under deciduous trees.

MECONOPSIS BETONICIFOLIA

Better known as M. Baileyi and perhaps the most striking introduction of the last half-century. From a clump of oval hairy leaves it raises several branching stems to 3-4 ft. and bears (June–July) poppy-flowers, 4 in. across, of a dazzling kingfisher-blue with a bold orange centre. A cool soil, well drained and enriched with leafy compost, with light shade. Easily raised from seed sown as soon as ripe. The plant is perennial if seedlings are induced to form off-sets by having their first flowering stems removed.

ANEMONE JAPONICA

ANEMONE PULSATILLA

ASTILBE KING ALBERT

One of the finest of the hybrid astilbes raising a sheaf of stems 6–7 ft. high, terminating in enormous fluffy panicles of white flowers. A hardy, easy plant in any rich, moist soil. Should be top-dressed in winter and divided every third or fourth year. Makes a fine background for some of the rich red varieties of only about half its stature.

ALLIUM TRIQUETRUM

Though apt to seed rather freely in the border, this is a charming plant for woodland, water-side or wild garden. About 8 in. high, it has the elegant poise of a wood hyacinth, and the white bells, in a leaning panicle, are each lined with green. In flower nearly all summer. May be grown in colonies from bulbs or seed, but better as a self-sown incident about uncultivated spots.

POLEMONIUM CARNEUM

The "Jacob's ladders" are generally blue, but this one is ivory-white with an overlay of salmon-rose. A very lovely plant, making a low mound of fern-like leaves over which the flowers (June–August) are carried on 12–18-in. branching stems. It offers no difficulty in a medium loam, not too dry, in sun or light shade. Clumps are the better for occasional division in autumn or spring. Rooted off-sets or seed.

POLYGONUM BISTORTA SUPERBA

TRILLIUM SESSILE

LILIUM BROWNII

The " Mystery Lily " is one of the most beautiful of its exalted family. It grows to some 3 ft., and the heavily textured blossoms, marble-white within and with maroon markings on the outside, are large and bold in line, yet beautifully proportioned and richly fragrant. Deep, freely drained soil, liberally mixed with ripe leaf compost and a little peat. Part shade is desirable, and a spring mulch of above compost and old manure is helpful. Division of bulbs or bulblets. Brownii Colchesteri often succeeds where the type does not.

ANEMONOPSIS MACROPHYLLA

PLATYCODON GRANDIFLORA MARIESII

IRIS TENAX

A delightful little iris of the Californian section, suitable for a rather dry, sandy loam (lime-free) with full sun. The stiff grassy leaves are grey-green, and the dainty flowers (June–July), rising to about 9 in., usually in some shade of lilac or lavender-blue. These blooms are yielded in great profusion, and the plant is quite hardy and long-lived in a really free soil. Division in spring, but, like most of this section, best raised from seed, which ripens freely.

LYSIMACHIA CLETHROIDES

GERANIUM ARMENUM

ASTRANTIA MAJOR

An attractive perennial for a shady border, woodland or between shrubs. From a leafy base it puts up branching stems terminating in full summer in round, many-rayed blossoms suggesting "everlastings." In colour these crisp and chaffy blooms are a blend of silver and vivid green with a gentle infusion of pink, and they are produced in luxuriance. Likes a cool, fairly stiff loam. Better for periodical lifting and division, its many off-sets providing ample material for increase.

A HYBRID ERIGERON

The erigerons are at their best as border plants in their many hybrids, whose broad-rayed, aster-like flowers are produced in succession throughout the later summer and autumn. In height they vary from 1 ft. to 2 ft., and they will flourish in any average soil, preferably to the light side, with a sunny aspect. A choice selection should include B. Ladhams, rosy amaranth; Elsie, rose-pink; Merstham Glory, violet-blue; Pink Pearl, flesh-pink; Quakeress, light mauve, also in white. Division in spring.

ASTER REMEMBRANCE

One of the taller members of a group of miniature Michaelmas daisies, so useful for a front row, this is also one of the most delightful. It makes a compact mass of about 1 ft. which is smothered in rosy-lavender blossoms (early October), these breaking from vivid pink buds. Will flourish in much lighter, drier soils than the average Michaelmas daisy and take care of itself indefinitely. Full sun essential. This variety not inclined to " run," but may be increased by rooted off-sets.

IRIS KAEMPFERI MORNING MIST

ANAPHALIS TRIPLINERVIS

LEUCOJUM ÆSTIVUM GRAVETYE

The summer snowflake follows L. vernum in May and continues until June. The Gravetye variety is the finest form, a plant of 18 in. with a bold tuft of grassy, dark green, glossy leaves and graceful heads of drooping bell-like flowers, pure white, the segments tipped with green. Will flourish and prove permanent in a medium soil, not too dry. Is at its best grouped between shrubs in the mixed border. Seems to enjoy light shade. Seed or division, but clumps doing well should not be disturbed.

ANEMONE TRIFOLIA

IRIS SIBIRICA

DAHLIA MERCKII

A charming little dahlia which is quite hardy in a free, gritty soil. It raises an 18-in. mass of typical dahlia leafage and over it on long slender stems are poised 2-in. single flowers. These, which prevail from August to first frost, are normally a soft rose-lilac, but may be of deeper or lighter shades. The place for this dainty plant is a sunny or lightly shaded bay in the shrub border. Easily raised from seed, or may be increased by division (tubers) in spring.

MECONOPSIS INTEGRIFOLIA

GERANIUM NEPALENSE

LILIUM SPECIOSUM

Although long grown as an indoor lily, this beautiful Japanese is quite hardy and easy in a well-drained soil, selecting a sunny nook in the mixed border where it may be grouped and left alone. The 3–4-ft. stems are rigid and the flowers beautifully reflexed, large, fragrant and extremely lasting when cut. Many varieties, of which the following are the choicest: L. s. album, pure white; Melpomene, crimson flecked with wine-red; rubrum, white suffused with crimson, spotted pink or carmine. Plant 8 in. deep in good bed of sandy loam with plenty of leafmould. Mulch with compost in late autumn. Seed.

ASTILBE GRANAT

A highly ornamental 3-ft. waterside or moist border perennial with foamy plumes (late summer) of richest ruby-crimson. In addition to those mentioned in the Plant List, its nearest rivals in the richer colours are William Reeves, crimson-scarlet; Mars, a taller grower in warm red; Fanal, raspberry-red; Freda Klapp, crimson-purple, one of the latest. All these are excellent varieties for providing the deep notes in a colour drift to lilac, rose, blush and white of these singularly beautiful plants. For cultural notes see p. 130.

£1